DISTANCING

DISTANCING

How Great Leaders Reframe
to Make Better Decisions

L. David Marquet
Michael A. Gillespie

PORTFOLIO ▶ PENGUIN

Portfolio / Penguin
An imprint of Penguin Random House LLC
1745 Broadway, New York, NY 10019
penguinrandomhouse.com

Most Portfolio books are available at a discount when purchased in quantity for sales promotions or corporate use. Special editions, which include personalized covers, excerpts, and corporate imprints, can be created when purchased in large quantities. For more information, please call (212) 572-2232 or email specialmarkets@ penguinrandomhouse.com. Your local bookstore can also assist with discounted bulk purchases using the Penguin Random House corporate Business-to-Business program. For assistance in locating a participating retailer, email B2B@penguinrandomhouse.com.

Book design by Alissa Rose Theodor

PORTFOLIO and PORTFOLIO with javelin thrower design are registered trademarks of Penguin Random House LLC.

ISBN 9780593713105 (hardcover)
ISBN 9780593713112 (ebook)

Printed in the United States of America
1st Printing

The authorized representative in the EU for product safety and compliance is Penguin Random House Ireland, Morrison Chambers, 32 Nassau Street, Dublin D02 YH68, Ireland, https://eu-contact.penguin.ie.

*To all who strive to make better decisions for a better world,
to reinvent themselves, to challenge the status quo,
and to lead more fulfilling lives.*

CONTENTS

FOREWORD

In my work with leaders across industries, one truth stands out:
The quality of decisions directly shapes the quality of outcomes.
In *The Right Decision Every Time*, I delved into the art of creating
clarity in high-stakes decision-making. What emerged as a central
theme is that clarity requires more than just information; it demands the ability to step back—to distance oneself from the emotions, biases, and noise that cloud judgment. Only through this
separation can leaders align their choices with their core values
and long-term goals. This is why I am profoundly excited about
Distancing, a book that not only deepens this understanding but
also provides a powerful framework for achieving it.

David Marquet and Michael Gillespie have crafted a work that
challenges us to think differently about decision-making and leadership. Drawing from David's transformative leadership aboard the
USS *Santa Fe*, chronicled in *Turn the Ship Around!*, and Mike's
deep expertise in organizational psychology, this book offers a powerful toolkit to intentionally achieve the needed psychological distance to break free from the biases and pressures that often hijack

our thinking. By stepping into someone else's shoes, viewing a situation from afar, or imagining the future self, the authors illuminate how to rise above the noise to think more clearly, lead more effectively, and decide with confidence.

What I Love About This Book

First of all, what makes this book especially compelling is its practicality. Distancing, a concept that might initially seem abstract, is rendered actionable through tangible tools and real-world examples. David and Mike demonstrate how distancing reframes problems, enabling leaders to pause, reflect, and make decisions not driven by the heat of the moment but by wisdom and alignment with core values.

Second, one of the most compelling aspects of this book is its emphasis on leadership in complex, high-stakes environments. As a CEO of a public company, I was faced with tough decisions that could make or break my company. In my conversations with executives, I heard the same concern: that just a couple of key decisions can change the whole trajectory of a company. David and Mike provide a road map to ensure those key decisions are right—thoughtful, intentional, and aligned with long-term success. They show us how distancing allows leaders to rise above immediate pressures to see the broader landscape, enabling clarity in the face of complexity.

Third, the book's insights are incredibly timely and critically important in today's world, where we are constantly inundated with information and demands. Leaders are expected to think quickly, yet the speed of modern life often comes at the expense of wisdom. This book offers a remedy: slowing down to create space for deeper thinking. As they show, the pause is not an interruption but a powerful tool for clarity and creativity.

Why You Want to Read This Book

This book is for everyone! It is not just a guide; it's an invitation to rethink how you think. It offers more than insights; it provides stories that bring these principles to life, from the control room of a nuclear submarine to corporate boardrooms to daily life. David and Mike's ability to weave together theory and practice makes this a transformative read for everybody.

I believe that *Distancing* will change the way you approach decision-making and leadership. It will equip you to face complexity with a new kind of confidence. As you turn these pages, you'll discover tools that will sharpen your focus, broaden your perspective, and deepen your impact.

David Marquet and Michael Gillespie have charted a bold new course in decision-making and leadership. If you are ready to lead with clarity, think with courage, and decide with confidence, this book is your guide. I encourage you to embark on this journey with curiosity and an open mind. The tools you'll gain will not only transform your leadership but also the lives of those you lead.

Here's to making better decisions—for ourselves, our organizations, and our world.

Luda Kopeikina
Author of *The Right Decision Every Time*
Boca Raton, Florida

DISTANCING

INTRODUCTION

Be *yourself. Be here now. Be in the moment.* We hear this advice constantly, in the media, from trusted experts and self-help gurus, and from well-meaning friends and family. The current zeitgeist considers the idea of "being present" as something to strive for, a state in which to exist at all times. On the surface, it seems like good advice: You'd want to be present—physically, mentally, and emotionally—while attending the graduation ceremony of your child, while working on an important project, or while enjoying the view after hiking to the summit of a mountain.

But sometimes we can be too immersed in our *me-here-and-now* selves, too locked in our own perspective. When someone says they "reacted on impulse" or "got caught up in the moment," the connotation is not positive. In fact, it often means they behaved in ways contrary to what was important to them and made decisions they later regretted. Tellingly, we can see this in others more easily than we can see it in ourselves. The fact is, "being present" isn't always what it's cracked up to be, especially when it comes to decision-making.

When excited, stressed, or threatened, we are pushed further into a state of self-immersion, a closed-in feeling of me-here-and-now, which narrows, filters, and distorts what we see, reinforcing our previously held beliefs. We can't see the forest for the trees. Our limited point of view biases our decisions toward what makes us feel good about ourselves, crippling our ability to weigh factors clearly. We restrict our range of options, and when we do decide, our decision is heavily influenced by the need to defend our egos. Sometimes, it paralyzes us. We continue with the status quo and miss wonderful new opportunities to grow, ultimately regretting the roads not taken.

We live in this immersed perspective and distorted reality, convinced that what we see, feel, need, and want to do are right. This immersed state is our default, by nature. We are, in effect, too close to ourselves. Our ego, biases, and emotions are all just too strong. They blind us to the best decisions and coax us into the comfortable ones. They lead us to favor decisions that make us look good and that validate our previous decisions and actions because, otherwise, that would mean we were wrong. This results not only in inferior decision-making but also in poor performance and, over time, a less fulfilling life. It can also spell disaster.

As a retired nuclear submarine captain, David had deep experience with command-and-control leadership structures. In his first book, *Turn the Ship Around!*, he told the story of how the USS *Santa Fe*, a nuclear-powered submarine with bitterly disappointing inspection results and a dispirited crew, dramatically reversed course.[1] By changing their language, taking small steps, and leveraging the powerful combination of communication and distributed decision ownership, the crew received the highest score in the history of the US Navy for operating their submarine, and morale soared. All thirty-three eligible sailors reenlisted over the next twelve months. Officers signed up to stay in the navy, and two withdrew their resignations. The most significant accomplishments happened after he departed. The ship continued to win a disproportionate number of awards, and ten officers were ultimately selected to command submarines—an unheard-of number.

He found himself giving speeches on every continent (except Antarctica) to companies that wanted to transform from leader-follower to leader-leader organizations, where the governing principle is to push authority to those with the information, not push information to those with the authority. This enabled teams to get the work done with high standards and significant autonomy while also aligning toward world-class performance.

His second book, *Leadership Is Language*, explored the difference between the Industrial Age language we've been programmed to speak that traps us in a follower mentality and an intent-based language that invites us instead to think like leaders and make decisions.[2] This intent-based approach emphasizes articulating our intentions—to ourselves and those around us—creating a bias toward action while naturally inviting input and more communication.

But his work was not complete. On the *Santa Fe*, the key was getting people to make decisions, but of course we needed good decisions, wise decisions. Often, he would see officers getting in their own way. It was not a case of insufficient information or the level of ambiguity and uncertainty, although these tended to trigger unhelpful states of mind, but rather their self-immersed state that seemed to blind them to obvious answers. If he asked a few questions—for example, What would you do if you were me? or What do you think the future you six months from now wishes you would do today?—they would immediately see clearly and arrive at better decisions. His clients were particularly interested in how this reframing improved decision-making.

Mike had spent years of research and practice on how to culti-
vate effective organizations and help people make better decisions.
His research about creating effective corporate cultures landed on
David's front porch in the form of a *Wall Street Journal* article.[3]
An organizational psychologist at the University of South Florida,
Mike also developed and directed an organization-wide critical
thinking program at the Sarasota-Manatee campus and conducted
workshops for business, government, and nonprofit organizations.
Participants consistently wanted to know how they could make
better decisions and help others do the same while having to deal
with real-time constraints.

David and Mike discovered that they were trying to solve the
same problem: How do we help people gain the necessary clarity
to make wise decisions to improve their own lives and help their
organizations? This book is a result of their collaboration, in which
they offer a simple yet powerful solution.

If being self-immersed is our default state, which distorts our
view of reality and results in poor decision-making, then we can
intentionally choose to exit self-immersion and take a distanced perspective. We need to get out of our typical ways of thinking, out
of our closed-off tendencies and biased worldviews. We need to step
away from the problem and remove ourselves from the situation so
we're able to look at it objectively—the way a coach might—and
decide what to do. Distance gives us the necessary perspective and
reframes the situation and the way we process it mentally so we can
make better decisions for ourselves and for our organizations. When
immersed, we are our practical selves. But when we are distanced,
we are more like our ideal selves, understanding which decisions
will best support and align with our values.

But how do we achieve this? Aren't we stuck with ourselves?
Yes, but with our powerfully imaginative and creative minds, we

can also choose to view the world from another's perspective. We introduce you to a mental technique called *psychological distancing* that enables you to exit your me-here-and-now self. Drawing on compelling scientific research, we explain why it works so well, and we show you three ways to do it: self-distancing, spatial distancing, and temporal distancing. First, you can *be someone else*, inhabiting another's perspective. This activates the neutral observer's outside point of view. Second, you can *be somewhere else*. You zoom out and see yourself from afar, as just another person who is part of a larger context. Third, you can *be sometime else*, imagining that you are your future self who is thinking back to what you wish you had done today. In each case, it feels like flipping a switch. By relocating your mind's eye, suddenly you see things you did not notice before, and you can coach yourself from this distanced perspective. Often, the answer appears instantly and seems obvious. This immediate reframe of how you see yourself and your situation radically improves the quality of your decision-making.

Seeing how powerful and effective distancing was in our own lives—it's like a superpower we never knew we had—over the years, we shared this technique with our clients and students. They, too, have reaped the benefits, achieving profound aha moments that led to better decisions, improved outcomes, and richer lives. We share some of their stories as well as business cases and useful exercises that will help you put this transformative technique into practice.

Before we get started, a few important caveats: Distancing is not merely about considering the viewpoint of others when making decisions or thinking about how a current action will affect your future self. While these are laudable, they are half steps because your perspective is still your own. You are casting your gaze further afield, but you are not exiting your immersed point of view.

The immersed self is the default state from which you see the world. It is not the same as ego, although egoic effects such as defensiveness, self-consciousness, and a focus on image are more active when in a self-immersed state. We think of the relationship between the immersed self and ego along the lines of oxygen and fire. The more immersed (oxygen) we are, the brighter the ego (fire) burns. The solution to reducing egoic effects is to take away the oxygen, which happens by exiting the immersed state.

The self-immersed state is not an extreme condition; it is our normal condition. As such, we are in it almost all the time. Like breathing, we don't think much about it. At the same time, we can be acutely mindful of our breathing during exercise, yoga, or meditation. Although we do this for only minutes a day, the benefits can accrue over our lifetime. In a similar way, we can activate a self-distanced state for a brief period in order to view the world through different eyes, see reality more clearly, develop a new insight, and make a better decision. But to execute that decision, we need to return to our normal, self-immersed state. And like mindful breathing, the benefits of regular practice accrue over time.

Now, let's take a look at how this plays out in a life-and-death situation, aboard Asiana Airlines Flight 214 with Captain Lee.

PART I

Two Perspectives

1

The Immersed Self

*Because we view ourselves and our worlds through
the eyes of our own egos, our perceptions are often
biased in ways that flatter ourselves.*

—PROFESSOR MARK LEARY

Saturday, July 6, 2013, was a clear afternoon with unlimited visibility over northern California. As they completed the eleven-hour flight from Seoul to San Francisco, the crew and passengers of Asiana 214 were treated to expansive midday views of the San Francisco Bay, the city skyline, and the Golden Gate Bridge. The Boeing 777 was nearly full, with 291 passengers, 12 flight attendants, and 4 flight crew members—a total of 307 people.[1]

In the cockpit, forty-five-year-old Captain Lee Kang-Kuk sat in the pilot's seat. Lee was a safe, experienced pilot with almost 10,000 total hours logged across various aircraft. He was moving up the ranks at Asiana, first to Boeing 737 captain in 2005 and then Airbus A320 captain in 2007. Now, six years later, he was being promoted to the larger Boeing 777. Over the past several months he had completed initial simulator training and accumulated thirty-three flight hours on the 777. This particular flight was an evaluation flight for full certification, under the supervision of a senior pilot.

That day, the electronic landing system at San Francisco International Airport (SFO) was out of service due to construction. This infrequent occurrence meant the flight crew would need to conduct a visual-only approach to the airport. They would be aided by a set of four landing lights alongside the runway, indicating the aircraft's vertical position relative to the desired three-degree glidepath. Each light shows either white or red. Four white means you are well above glidepath; two white and two red signal you are on track. The more red lights, the farther you are below the glidepath. Four red lights trigger a critical decision: whether to try to save the landing or to abort.

Visual-only approaches are considered business as usual for professional pilots, especially with a cloudless, sunny sky like there was that day. A plane a minute had been landing under these conditions at SFO throughout the morning without problems. But while Captain Lee had completed two manual, visual-only approaches in the simulator, this would be his first in an actual 777 full of passengers. Lee was stressed by this but did not tell anyone—not ahead of the flight, nor during the required approach briefing.

As Asiana 214 neared SFO, its initial approach was high. Lee responded by increasing the descent rate. He announced that he was going to fully extend the flaps, which would slow the plane, but they were going too fast for full flaps. A mistake, and he was overridden by his evaluator.

Lee held off as instructed. But then in his next effort to manage the descent, he mispositioned a switch on the autopilot. The plane unexpectedly accelerated and climbed, putting the approach even farther above the desired glidepath. The evaluator noted this mistake as well. Lee manually reduced engine speed to idle, inadvertently disabling the autopilot's control of the engine speed. The pilots were silent on this change—and its implication for thrust control to maintain minimum airspeed.

When the landing lights came into view, it was bad news: four white. Many control inputs, little communication, and no closer to being on track. The evaluator noted they were high, but no one dared announce four whites. By now, however, the plane was dropping fast to compensate as its engines sat idle and its airspeed slowed below the preset landing target of 137 knots, unnoticed by both the pilot and the evaluator. Lee thought the autopilot would maintain airspeed. Instead, with engine power remaining idle due to the manual override, airspeed fell as low as 103 knots.

The landing lights started changing. Fast. First one red, then two, then three, culminating in all four red. This transition from four white to four red happened in less than thirty seconds.

By this point, Lee and the evaluator had several indications things were amiss. The plane was not flying as expected, first climbing unexpectedly and now losing speed and altitude at twice the target rate. The engines were still at idle. Yet during this time, there were long periods of silence in the cockpit, punctuated by short, stiff reports between the pilots. At no time did Lee ask for help or say he was confused by what was happening.

Instead, the pilots tried to convince themselves everything was under control. The evaluating pilot reassuringly announced the plane was "on track," choosing to note the few seconds when the lights showed two white and two red as it transitioned from above to below glidepath to affirm everything was fine. This suited Lee well, as he was acutely aware that four red lights would signal that he was failing his exam. Lee reported he never saw these indications of failure. The plane was bound for the bay, short of the runway. And still, silence.

With the evaluator focused on reassuring data and Lee rejecting distressing data, both were slow to react. At two hundred feet above the runway—which sits nearly at sea level on the water's edge—and fifteen seconds before impact, the evaluating pilot reported, "It's low." Even then, Captain Lee hesitated to power up the engines, abort the landing, and go around. This was the last opportunity to save the plane.

The delay proved fatal. At one hundred feet, the evaluating pilot took over and applied full throttle. It was too late. The tail of the plane struck the seawall and broke off. Asiana Flight 214 had crashed, killing three passengers. It was the first fatal crash to involve a Boeing 777.

An engineering reconstruction showed that if the go-around had been attempted even four seconds earlier, the crash could have been averted.

Why did this happen?

Me, Myself, and Ego

The answer is not that Captain Lee was a bad pilot. Available evidence leading up to the fateful day points to the contrary. The answer is that Lee is human and subject to the same human foibles we all are. His hidden fears, his need to appear that he had everything under control leading up to and during the flight, and his focus on passing the evaluation rather than on landing the plane safely were all manifestations of the defensiveness that accompanies one's ego under conditions of threat.

The immediate answer is that he did not execute a go-around when needed. Why not? Because he never saw the four red lights. Why didn't he see them? Because he was so focused on not failing the exam. Ultimately, he was too immersed in his own perspective and how the landing would affect him. That threat to self triggered a defensive mentality that hijacked his focus from landing the plane safely to not looking bad. It also overly anchored him on his initial mental model that the autopilot was maintaining speed, although it was not. He was committed to figuring out *how* to land the plane instead of elevating his thinking to *whether* he should land the plane in the first place.

Mark Leary is a social and personality psychologist who studies the self and the problems it causes us. In his book *The Curse of the Self,* he asserts that the primary cause of our unhappiness is not our circumstances or what others do to us, but the self.[2] Our concept of self is our sense of being an autonomous, unique, separate organism in the world, with our own identity, values, and dreams and the ability to chart a course to achieve them. *Ego,* which is the Latin word for "I," refers to this sense of self. In everyday language, *ego* is often used in a pejorative way, something to blame for the negative effects that come from self-awareness.

It is one thing to possess the capacity for self-awareness, but another to have too great an emphasis on the self, or to be too mired in one's own ego. Jordan Peterson is a keen-witted, often-polarizing Canadian psychologist who routinely offers his commentaries on psychological topics of public interest. In a podcast with comedian Theo Von, Peterson talks about the perils of too much self-referential thinking.[3] He claims that it is possible to identify those who are depressed or psychotic with 75 percent accuracy, based on how much self-referential content is in their writing. He goes on to say that the more you think about yourself, the worse you feel, and that the antidote to social anxiety is to focus on other people instead. In other words, get out of your own head.

Of course, the self is not inherently bad. Leary catalogs many of the benefits it affords us as a species. The self carries with it the capacity for self-reflection, or our ability to conceptualize us as an entity, distinct from the world around us. This ability to self-reflect enables humans to plan, deliberate, think introspectively, evaluate others and ourselves, and exercise self-control while providing the motivation to adjust our behavior to align with who we want to be or what we want to achieve. Having a self gives us an awareness that we are responsible for our actions. These attributes have allowed humans to multiply and take over the planet.

Though these characteristics are beneficial from an evolutionary perspective, Leary points out a dark side: We worry about how others perceive us. Our ability to evaluate ourselves and other people means we recognize that as we evaluate others, others evaluate us. This has the perverse impact of motivating us to *look* good at the expense of actually *being* good.[4]

Especially under conditions of threat, ego is problematically concerned about image. In his book *The Righteous Mind*, social psychologist Jonathan Haidt calls ego our "in-house press secretary."[5] When engaged, ego is our built-in defender and promoter, with one agenda: to make us look good and feel good about ourselves. It does so by curating reality even before it reaches our perception. In everyday conversation, when we say someone has a big ego or that their ego is getting in the way, we are emphasizing the less favorable characteristics of our sense of self. These dysfunctional features of ego lead to defensiveness, arrogance, insecurity, and fragility, and they distort our view of reality. It may be useful to think about these dysfunctional features of ego as being engaged or disengaged.

Once this so-called ego is engaged, our focus is hijacked from the task at hand to the image we display. Ego selectively focuses and filters what the brain pays attention to in an effort to support looking good. Our engaged ego biases our decision-making toward those choices that protect our identity, including affirming previous decisions we have made.

The unfortunate result is that we are stuck in *how* thinking. *How* to think or act in support of ego's agenda—how to land the plane, in the Captain Lee example—when we would be better off thinking *what*, *whether*, or *why*: Should we even land the plane? This lower level of thinking is limiting. As our motive shifts from task performance to image management, our brain conveniently ensures that any preconceived notions we hold are likely to stand—perceptually at least—as it seeks confirming information and avoids any conflicting data. We focus on a string of inputs that convinces us we are right. This is called *confirmation bias*. We have a distorted view of reality, which we become quite certain is the only correct view.

The reality distortion effect is so strong that it has the power to literally blind us. Captain Lee reported that he "never saw the four red lights." Since a complete view of reality would be overwhelming and confusing, our brains are constantly choosing what to pay attention to and what to ignore—and they are filling in the blanks for what is unseen and unknown. Indications that show us as competent, consistent, good people living in alignment with our values are fast-tracked to our consciousness. Those that show us as incompetent and inconsistent are, well, best ignored. This willful blindness largely happens automatically, instantly, and effortlessly.

In our daily lives, this distortion manifests as "I never said that," even when we did, or "You never told me that," even when they did. These distortions happen to us all the time. As the late behavioral psychologist Daniel Kahneman described in *Thinking, Fast and Slow,* "What we see is all there is."[6] When the brain filters out information that is right before our eyes, it is treated as if it does not exist.

Willful blindness happens more frequently than you might think. Author Margaret Heffernan has written a book on the phenomenon, *Willful Blindness: Why We Ignore the Obvious at Our Peril,* about how we choose not to see.[7] Wives not seeing their husband's infidelity; investors in Madoff's funds not seeing that the returns he was reporting were most likely fraudulent; Germans not seeing the concentration camp in the forest near their town.

Further, our decision-making calculus is biased toward being consistent with our previous decisions. We double down on our past actions and choices because we have incorporated them into our identity. This is the sunk-cost fallacy, in which we refuse to veer from a strategy or action once it's already underway because we feel invested in it. We are prone to this escalation of commitment to a failing course of action. We tend to maintain the path we've previously chosen because, after all, we are the ones who chose it, and we believe we are right. It's all part of a misguided pattern of behavior that protects us from all manner of perceived threats.

This is a real problem with deadly consequences. A study by Carnegie Mellon's Binyamin Cooper and colleagues measured the effects of rudeness on anchoring.[8] *Anchoring* is a common decision-making bias describing the condition whereby we tend to get stuck on a single piece of information, often the first piece of information, when making a decision. This affects everything from judgments about daily activities to negotiations. Anchoring is a very common—some studies suggest it is the most common—decision bias affecting errors in medicine. The doctor walks into a room and the nurse suggests heart attack. That diagnosis will stubbornly persist in the mind of the doctor despite disconfirming evidence. In the study, fourth-year medical students were invited into an emergency room simulation requiring diagnosis of a patient presenting with chest discomfort. The patient's daughter said she was worried about her father having a heart attack (the anchor). However, the correct diagnosis was acid reflux.

On the way to see the patient a random subset of the participants witnessed an act of rudeness to another person. Students exposed to rudeness were more likely to stick with the initial, incorrect diagnosis (heart attack) despite receiving further diagnostic information that should have led them to the correct conclusion. In contrast, those in the control group were better able to shift away from the incorrect initial diagnosis.

Self-Protection

For a species to survive, it needs to protect itself from damage, whether from the environment, predators, or other external factors. The pain system within organisms is at the front line of this protection. It's what sends a signal to the brain that something is dangerous or causing injury: a poisonous plant, a hungry lion, a raging fire. In humans, this signal is received by pain-sensitive nerves and transmitted to our brain via the spinal column and the nervous system. When pain is perceived, we react physically. Typically, this reaction involves some sort of motion or preparation for motion: We jerk our hand away. We fight back. We run.

Most senses, such as smell, dull themselves in response to consistent exposure. This is not the case for pain. Enter a room with a particularly foul smell, and after a while, you don't notice it. Well, not as much, anyway. Say you live by the railroad tracks. In time, you no longer pay attention to the sound of the trains lumbering by. But pain may amplify if the source is not removed, and though you can train yourself to tolerate pain and react differently—not pull your arm away when receiving a shot—the sensation is still there. You can't train yourself to feel less physical pain.

Like physical pain, social pain is sensed and passed to the brain for action. As social animals, we evolved to have a strong desire to be part of the tribe. For much of our existence, getting kicked out of our tribe meant death, so we are sensitive to social threats: an askance glance, exclusion from an activity, isolation from the group.[9] Since the brain already had a system for processing physical pain, it was evolutionarily expedient to process social pain using the same pathways. Social pain is similarly alleviated by a physical response. And like physical pain, social pain doesn't mitigate with exposure. Training ourselves to reinterpret social pain signals is a slow and effortful process. It feels like we are going against our nature—because we are.

To understand the connection between social and physical pain, we have an unlikely starting point. An unassuming yet intensely curious researcher, Jaak Panksepp, made the droll discovery that rats laugh when tickled.[10] This research was *not* immediately welcomed in his scientific community. Panksepp was pushing against the dominant current of behaviorism. You remember behaviorism: One of its most famous examples was Pavlov's dog.

Panksepp thought the behaviorists had gone too far in rejecting the role of emotions and reducing all human and animal activity to a set of conditioned responses to stimuli. He believed emotions played an important role in joy, suffering, and daily activity. In a set of creative and unprecedented experiments, Panksepp tickled rats, detecting squeaks and chirps at frequencies above what humans can hear unaided. The rats were laughing.

In a 1977 study at Bowling Green University, he and Barbara Herman measured the social pain of young guinea pigs being separated from their mothers by the number of distressed squeaks they made.[11] Guinea pigs given morphine, a drug designed to mask physical pain, squeaked less, implying they felt less social pain.

Since then, a growing body of work has confirmed the finding that our brains process social pain in a way that looks similar to how our brains process physical pain. A 2010 study took functional magnetic resonance imaging (fMRI) readings as students played a virtual ball-toss game.[12] Subjects thought they were playing with two other humans in the study, but they were actually playing with preprogrammed computer "players." The computer players included the subjects in the game for a while and then excluded them. When that happened, the fMRI readings showed brain activity in the same places that indicate physical pain. The same study found that a simple physical pain medication, Tylenol, reduced that same brain region's reactivity to the social pain of being excluded. In other words, when our feelings are hurt, our brains experience that social pain in a way that is similar to the experience of physical pain.

This same team ran another study with two groups of students who completed a journaling activity for three weeks. Half were randomly assigned to take a daily Tylenol, and the other half took a placebo. They all completed a nightly survey on how easily they felt hurt by others or how resilient they were to criticism or other social threats. They were asked to agree or disagree with statements like "Being teased hurts my feelings." Again, the Tylenol worked. Those who were in the daily dose group reported greater resilience and lower social pain.

Though there are similarities between the processing of physical pain and social pain, there are also differences. For example, we can continually reexperience social pain but not physical pain.[13] You can recall the situation where you experienced physical pain, but you don't reexperience the actual hurt. With social pain, we can both recall the situation and reexperience the hurt. So, we're further motivated to protect ourselves from social pain.

Our response to social threat is a direct extension of our response to physical threat, which is hardwired in us. We are naturally programmed to avoid threats to our identity, threats to our ego. Therefore, we are, to a certain degree, stuck with ego. Perhaps this is why philosophers, psychologists, religious leaders, and writers throughout time have all been so persistently trying to solve the problem of ego. Sure, there are useful lessons to be learned, but we keep coming back to the same core problem. The key to disengaging the dysfunctional effects of ego is not to try to attack it directly but to understand better the perceptual state under which ego is likely to be activated. That condition is called the immersed self.

Self-Immersion Is Our Default

Put yourself in Captain Lee's position. You are a professional pilot. It is a major part of your identity. Now, you have been selected for promotion to 777 captain. Your job is to pass this evaluation flight with your reputation intact. You are focused on *yourself* and *your* performance. You see everything through a self-conscious, evaluative lens. Your perception narrows. Don't screw up. You have a rocky start with extending the flaps and operating the autopilot. Two demerits. You are nervous. You don't question aloud why the autopilot did what it did; you just adjust for it manually and press on with the landing.

You feel like you've recovered. But as the landing lights come into view, they show four white, confirming what you already know.

You are way too high. But then the lights start changing faster than you have ever seen before. Almost immediately three red appear. You are stressed, anxious, and scared. Now you are really worried about failing your exam. Your focus remains steadfastly on landing the plane rather than on *whether* to land the plane this time or go-around.

Rapidly expanding in your mind is an awareness that four red lights will spell failure. You do not want to see four red. Your brain accommodates. Seconds later, when the lights do go to four red, your brain filters out this highly disturbing information. You never see four red. During these moments, you think this landing will determine your reputation forever, not to mention the course of your entire career, your entire life even. It is all that matters. You are excruciatingly, debilitatingly self-conscious. Everything collapses into this feeling that it is all about *me*, right *here*, right *now*. This is what it's like to be self-immersed.

The immersed self is our default state. We are our primary point of reference, the protagonists in our own stories. We live inside our heads, stuck in a myopic first-person point of view wherein—problematically—our emotions cloud our thinking, and we are unable to separate our thoughts from our feelings. When asked to describe our feelings, we use *I*, *me*, and *my* pronouns automatically. When asked to locate our sense of *self*, most people—especially in Western cultures—point to an area behind and slightly above the eyeballs. Looking at the world from our perspective, from behind our own eyes, we think of things as happening to *me*. All physical distance is relative to where I am, *here*, and all time is anchored by *now*. This me-here-and-now frame is the experience of the immersed self.

We are biased toward this me-here-and-now perspective and to things like us. In one interesting study about what languages sound "prettiest" to us,[14] researchers looked at language groups, how nasal the vowels were, the presence of particular consonant sounds like *sh* or *ch*, tonality, and rhythm. In general, participants scored all languages fairly similarly, negating both the hypothesis about how some languages (French, say) sound prettier than others (like the more guttural German). There was one strong correlation, however. We like languages we are familiar with more, giving them an average of a 12 percent boost in score.

The more self-immersed we are, the more selective our brain becomes. The result is that our blind spot, which hides our incompetence or inconsistencies, gets increasingly bigger. Because of this attentional selection, this immersed state feels closed in. Tunnel vision takes hold. We become more locked in to seeing the world from only our perspective. The net effect is to become more self-immersed—a vicious cycle.

We experience this sense of self-immersion most strongly in situations when we feel most vulnerable—we are being tested or evaluated, or we feel insulted, ignored, or invisible, especially in a public setting. You trip awkwardly as you walk up to greet a friend. You immediately become self-conscious and wonder, How did that look? No doubt you have felt this before. (Interestingly, the opposite—lavish praise—has the same immersive effect.)

When under stress, the immersed perspective is magnified. The pressure of an upcoming deadline, a critical review of our work (especially a public one), judgment by a spouse or loved one, or a threat to our social status—these common situations lock us more fully in this state. Someone cuts us off on the road, criticizes our presentation, threatens our position at work, or even asks us why we did something the way we did it—immediately our perceptions narrow, and our thinking does not extend beyond the moment. Road rage may follow, or we might dismiss or resent feedback. No matter our response, it comes from a point of obfuscation, not clarity. When we're on the defense, we're unable to think into even the near future, and our ability to make good decisions tends to disappear.

While the immersed self allows us to think of ourselves as an integrated and stable entity, distinct from others and unique in this world—having a history, feelings and emotions, and hopes and plans for the future—self-immersion at the wrong time can be disastrous. We become protective, especially of our identity, whether as a capable pilot, good parent, friendly coworker, or however we see ourselves. This can extend to people and groups we identify with. It is the self-immersed state that makes us ask, Why is this happening *to me?* and makes us feel that *I* am the center of *my* own universe.

We take this state so much for granted that we rarely stop to think that there are other ways to see the world.

THE IMMERSED SELF AS INVESTOR

If you are an active trader, there is a high probability that your portfolio is underperforming the market. There is also a high probability that you will deny this fact to yourself. This is because our minds curate reality, highlighting our wins and minimizing our losses. While there can be outliers for short periods of time, the evidence is clear and overwhelming. Most active investors underperform the market. The more people muck around with their investments, the worse they do. Instead, most of us would be better off investing in a broad market index fund and doing nothing at all.[15]

In financial circles, the *return gap* or the *investor gap* is the difference between what the investment returns and what a typical investor in that investment receives. It should be the same, right? It is not. For example, a mutual fund might return 10 percent in a year, but the typical investor in that fund achieves only a 9 percent return. How can this be? Because individual investors have a habit of selling once panic sets in and prices are low, and then buying once exuberance strikes and prices are high. The 1 percent gap in this example is typical. It might seem small, but that 1 percent is the difference between the investor's $100,000 growing to $1.33 million or $1.75 million over thirty years.

Derek Horstmeyer, a professor of finance at George Mason University, conducted an analysis of how market conditions affected investor decisions.[16] In down markets and more volatile periods, this gap was bigger. Although the gap may vary depending on the type of investment, say, international growth stocks or domestic value stocks, here's the most important lesson: The gap is always negative.

Highly volatile years, such as during the COVID-19 pandemic or the financial crisis, play the most havoc on our investing behavior. Horstmeyer reports, "Volatility seems to induce poor decisions in investors—people tend to get spooked at the bottom and abandon their positions, and then enter back into the positions when the market has already rebounded. . . . Market timing is almost always a loser. But it's especially a loser in high-volatility years."

We know there are psychological reasons for this. We feel anxious during periods of volatility when stock prices are fluctuating wildly up and (especially) down. This anxiety creates stress, and that stress pushes us into a self-immersed state. We lose the big picture and are more prone to making bad decisions. During periods of market volatility, it would be best to take a page from Odysseus's playbook. He tied himself to the mast of his ship and forbade his crew from following his orders to release him as they sailed past the Sirens.

This behavior spills over into professional investment management as well. Investors can choose between mutual funds, which rely on the professional judgment of a fund manager, and an exchange-traded fund (ETF), which automatically tracks a segment, industry, or entire market. A recent study covering 7,800 mutual funds over the past three decades showed the cost of investing in mutual funds instead of passive ETFs to be $1 trillion of lost wealth to investors.[17] The reason is threefold. First, investors choose the wrong times to buy and sell, essentially buying high and selling low. Second, fund managers are forced to do the same, as they have to sell stocks at depressed prices to cover the redemptions investors are making and to buy high to deploy the new cash investors are putting into the funds. Last, active mutual fund managers on average underperform the passive ETF because costs are higher and the professionals do not overperform the market by a large enough degree to compensate for the extra costs.

The American Association of Individual Investors (AAII) conducts a weekly survey of investors, who indicate whether they think the market will be higher, lower, or about the same in six months. The difference between those who think the market will be higher (bulls) and lower (bears) provides an indication, but it is a contrarian signal.[18]

When most investors think the market will go up, they have invested their money accordingly, and there is less money to enter the market and drive it higher. Therefore, the market actually is nearing a peak. At the same time, if most investors think the market will go down, they have withdrawn their money accordingly, and there is more money to reenter the market. Therefore, the market actually is nearing a bottom. The share prices will already reflect the impact of the money withdrawals or additions. Therefore, when most investors express a sentiment that the market will go up, it ought to, on average, go down.

This is indeed the case. The AAII website states: "The Sentiment Survey is a contrarian indicator. Above-average market returns have often followed unusually low levels of optimism, while below-average market returns have often followed unusually high levels of optimism." Most individual investors are wrong about market predictions. They are wrong, even knowing a thirty-seven-year history that most people are wrong. The point is not that AAII members are bad investors but that they are human. The aggregation of these human judgments combined with the economic implications of their decision results in a contrarian market signal.

Jason Zweig writes "The Intelligent Investor" weekly column for *The Wall Street Journal*. He worked with Daniel Kahneman on *Thinking, Fast and Slow*, so he knows a thing or two about human biases. Zweig sits at the intersection of our self-delusions and investing. He asks readers of his column to predict where the market, interest rates, commodities, and crypto currencies will go for the next year. At the end of 2021, they predicted the S&P (Standard & Poor's) 500, a broad market index, would rise 6 percent. In December 2022, he asked them to recall what they had predicted. Their recollections were consistently off, and collectively, they recalled predicting a drop of 1 percent. How could they have been so bad at remembering what they had predicted? Well, the market at that time was down 15 percent. Not only were they wrong about the direction of the market, but they were also wrong about being wrong![19]

We think we are better investors, drivers, etc., than we are—the so-called self-serving bias. We are aware of this from a classic 1981 study in which 93 percent of American drivers rated themselves as having above average or better driving skills compared to other drivers, even though this is by far a statistical impossibility.[20] Drivers with a history of serious accidents and traffic violations have comparable self-ratings as those without such a history. Experience, it seems, is not sufficient to overcome these biases.

In the case of investments, there is an unambiguous price signal about whether your decision to buy or sell a certain stock was a good one. It is clear, measurable, and visible. Yet, we are still able to delude ourselves. Like Captain Lee, our brains do not want us to see the four red lights.

Choose to Exit Self-Immersion

You might ask, Well, what viewpoint should I be using other than my own? It helps to first understand that our viewpoint is not static. We can exit our self-immersed state and choose another point of view. We have the ability to step outside ourselves and manipulate our perspective. We can imagine ourselves as someone else—an objective coach, a neutral observer—take that persona's point of view, and see ourselves from a distance. When we do this, we disengage our ego and are liberated from the need to defend and protect our thoughts and emotions because we no longer see them as our own. This distanced perspective enables us to see far more clearly and to make better decisions.

So, the core actionable problem is not that we have this thing we call an ego; it is that we live in a state of self-immersion by default. Trying to solve our problems with ego is a long fraught road. Exiting the immersed self, however, immediately disengages us from the dysfunctions of ego. Once we exit self-immersion, we are no longer the "I" that needs defending.

We may not realize that we have a choice to exit our immersed self, but we do. This simple act is one of the most powerful things we can do to make better decisions, avoid disastrous ones, and lead a more fulfilling life.

2

The Distanced Self

*If we got kicked out and the board brought in a
new CEO, what do you think he would do?*

—ANDY GROVE TO GORDON MOORE

In the early 1980s, there was an air of optimism in the United
States. Paul Volcker, the chair of the Federal Reserve at the time,
had licked inflation, and the stock market was rising after seven-
teen years of going sideways. Madonna and Michael Jackson were
burning up the charts, and a new TV station focused on music
videos was revolutionizing the entertainment industry and youth
culture.

But at Intel, CEO Gordon Moore and president Andrew Grove
were not along for the ride. Their 1985 annual report opened
with, "It was a miserable year for Intel and the semiconductor industry."[1] Both Moore and Grove had been with the company
since its inception in 1968, Moore as cofounder and Grove as head
of engineering. Since then, they had built Intel into a highly successful tech behemoth with twenty-three thousand employees and
$1.6 billion annual revenue (about $4.6 billion in 2024 dollars).

Moore and Grove could rightly be proud of the company they
had built. Their decisions, designs, and approach in running Intel
had made the pair wealthy and famous, at least in Silicon Valley

and the wider business world. Additionally, Moore was a technology thought leader known for "Moore's law," which postulated that the number of transistors on an integrated circuit doubles every two years.

Intel's success rested on its main product: memory chips, an essential component of every computer. But they had also developed the 4004 microprocessor. While memory chips store data, microprocessors process it, analyzing inputs and information. They are more complicated, expensive, and harder to manufacture. Although a small part of the company's business, the 4004 had been commercially successful. What was pressuring Intel, however, was that the market for memory chips had become commoditized. Competition on price and quality from Japanese and Korean manufacturers shrank Intel's revenues and reduced earnings to nearly zero.

Moore and Grove had a decision to make: stick with memory chips or shift their firm to microprocessors. The company did not have the resources to do both. The decision would determine the future and fate of the company.

For a year, Moore and Grove debated what to do. Despite the uncertainty, it seemed like a straightforward strategic decision to go all-in on microprocessors. The complex design and manufacture would play to the strength of the company's technological prowess, and Intel had already demonstrated their capabilities with the 4004. The IBM personal computer (PC) was built with Intel's microprocessor, and the demand for IBM PCs was increasing, along with the proliferation of additional PC manufacturers, which also used the Intel microprocessor. In fact, they could not keep up with demand. Nevertheless, Moore and Grove were paralyzed. They maintained the status quo—in essence, deciding by not deciding. They could not bring themselves to walk away from their legacy product.

As Grove explained, "Our priorities were formed by our identity; after all, memories were us."[2] Based on years of experience, the people of Intel, including Moore and Grove, had two strongly held beliefs about how their business ran and how to be successful. First, memory chips were the technological driver of all their products. Second, Intel needed to offer clients a full product line, which would always include memory chips. Because of these beliefs, the only acceptable question at Intel was, How are we going to make memory chips?, not What should we make? Their decision-making was unnecessarily restricted to the concrete choices around *how* they should make memory chips, not *whether* they should make memory chips.

Even when they allowed themselves to ask the question in an abstract way, their minds could not seriously entertain any answer other than continuing as a memory chip company. It was just too painful to walk away from their flagship product. The attachment was too strong, and it would have meant admitting that somewhere in the past, they had made a wrong turn.

Then, in one meeting, Grove posed a hypothetical question: "If we were replaced, what would our replacements do?" Instantaneously, with this reframe, the answer became clear. Grove tells the story:

> I remember a time in the middle of 1985, after this aimless wandering had been going on for almost a year. I was in my office with Intel's chairman and CEO, Gordon Moore, and we were discussing our quandary. Our mood was downbeat. I looked out the window at the Ferris wheel of the Great America

amusement park revolving in the distance, then I turned back to Gordon and asked, "If we got kicked out and the board brought in a new CEO, what do you think he would do?" Gordon answered without hesitation, "He would get us out of memories." I stared at him, numb, then said, "Why shouldn't you and I walk out the door, come back and do it ourselves?"[3]

In 1985, Intel shifted focus to producing microprocessors. That same year, C++ launched, Nintendo came out, and Michael Dell founded his PC company. The computer revolution was on.

The Reframe

When Moore and Grove metaphorically walked out the door and came back as "their replacements," they each exited their self-immersed state, became someone else, and looked at their situation from a distance. That neutral and objective perspective allowed them to detach from their ego, along with the need to defend it and all their past decisions. They dispelled the social threat and the threat to their identity by removing the oldest and most persistent barrier to seeing the situation clearly: themselves.

After being stuck for a year, the jump to the self-distanced state resulted in a flash of insight, triggered by frustration and a gaze out the window at a Ferris wheel. The distanced perspective instantly unlocked the answer to their problem.

In the self-distanced state we have an objective, external, third-person view from which we see ourselves and our situation without bias. By temporarily removing ourselves from the singular first-person point of view, which is inextricably informed by our memories, prejudices, hopes, and hurts, we are able to see and think more clearly, unencumbered by our personal experiences and feelings—and our need to look good or defend ourselves. The distanced self is not preoccupied with image preservation but is focused on the task. In this state, we are open, aware, relaxed, and curious. This creates a clarity that is often lost in a world where it is all about me, myself, and I. The distanced self is the opposite of egocentric. There's no need for the distanced self to be defensive because, well, that wasn't *me* making those decisions, so I am not attached to them.

This approach may seem to fly in the face of a popular sentiment, in which we are often urged to "be yourself," "be present," or "be in the moment"—but if we are present in the moment while being self-immersed, we can lose sight of the bigger picture, unnecessarily restrict our freedom of choice, fail to notice we are passively deciding, or just plain make the wrong decision.

Distance Changes How We Think

Distance changes the way we think about a given situation, problem, or decision. Like Moore and Grove who imagined they were their replacements, we achieve this distance from ourselves mentally. This is called psychological distance. The science at play here draws from construal level theory (CLT), which describes a pattern of how we think about things or how we mentally construe them. Lower levels of construal result in thinking concretely about details and *how* to do something. Higher levels of construal result in thinking abstractly about principles and *what*, *whether*, or *why* we do something. Captain Lee was thinking at a low level of construal: stuck on how to land the plane. Moore and Grove were also stuck at a low construal level: how best to make memory chips. Here's the rule: Greater psychological distance invites higher levels of construal. Once Moore and Grove each distanced by imagining they were someone else, they moved to a higher construal level, and the question of whether they should be making memory chips became salient.

Higher levels of construal also focus on desirability, or an ideal end state, as opposed to mere feasibility. This kind of thinking is characterized by greater flexibility and self-control and is more resistant to temptation and manipulation.

A self-immersed mind thinks, *How* do I land the plane? whereas a self-distanced one asks, *Should* I land the plane? Here are some differences between low-level and high-level construal.

CONSTRUAL LEVEL

LOW	HIGH
Concrete	Abstract
Practical	Ideal
Near (self, space, time)	Far (self, space, time)
Focus on *how*	Focus on *what, why, whether*
About me	About someone
Closer	Farther
Sooner	Later
Poor emotional regulation	Good emotional regulation
More susceptible to temptation	Less susceptible to temptation
More shame over past events	Less shame over past events
Poorer decisions	Wiser decisions

It's not that a higher or lower level of construal is better; it's that we need to match our level of construal to what we are trying to do. Making a decision? Invoke a higher level of construal for perspective and distance. Need project progress? Then get practical with a lower level of construal.

Yaacov Trope of New York University and Nira Liberman of Tel Aviv University developed CLT to explain why people think at widely different levels of abstraction and mental horizons and to help people transcend the egocentric concerns of the here and now.[4] The professors' solution is to change how we mentally construe an event or decision, whether we think about low-level details or a big-picture, more abstract purpose. The bigger the picture and the more abstract the purpose, the more our mental horizons broaden.

Liberman and Trope's initial study looked specifically at the time dimension—*temporal distance*, which is how far away something is from us in time.[5] Their work builds on the human bias known as *temporal discounting*. This means that as time moves forward, each additional increment of time starts to matter less and less. For example, the difference between now and a week from now feels much bigger than between fifty-two and fifty-three weeks from now, even though the time distance is the same in both scenarios. This causes us to disproportionately value what's happening now and in the immediate future more than what will happen in the distant future. The study also showed that when people think about events or issues as further away in time, they focus more on the *why* or the *what* to do, rather than on the *how*.

Participants were given a list of activities, such as "caring for houseplants," and then asked to write open-ended statements describing those activities either tomorrow or a year from now. Responses were scored based on the level of thinking. More abstract, higher-level construal would be represented by language that fit the pattern "[description] by [given activity]." For example, "I make the room look nice by caring for houseplants" indicated high-level construal thinking. A more concrete, low-level construal statement would reverse that pattern, so "[given activity] by [description]."

For example, "I care for houseplants by watering them" indicated low-level construal thinking. When describing activities for a year from now, people wrote more abstract sentences. When describing activities for tomorrow, they wrote more concrete sentences. Liberman and Trope elaborated their theory to include other ways in which we can access higher levels of construal beyond that of temporal distance: self/social distance and spatial distance. *Self-distance*, similar to social distance from a social-psychological perspective, refers to taking a perspective that is not our own, such as when Moore and Grove took the perspective of their replacements. *Spatial distance* refers to taking a position physically removed from us in space, such as imagining (or viewing) what the earth looks like from the moon, or seeing our own yard from the perspective of our neighbor's.

By manipulating *who*, *where*, and *when*, we create (or reduce) psychological distance, with greater distance leading to higher levels of thought abstraction. These dimensions of distance are linked and mutually reinforcing. For example, when we imagine being in a different location, we may also feel like we become someone else. And distant in time feels far away. They go together—long ago and far away.

To make better decisions, we need to be able to think in a distanced manner. From afar, we are able to get out of the weeds, to focus on what's important, and to think in terms of *why* and *what*. Detailed, in-the-moment execution of the *how* is necessary—for instance, when hiking along a trail with a steep drop-off, we want to pay attention to our foot placement, or when pushing through the execution phase of a large project, we want to focus on the details of each stage. But to make better decisions in life, about work, relationships, or the future, or when we're inviting and processing feedback, the bigger-picture *why* and *what* perspective is more effective. We can deliberately exit self-immersion and create self-distance when needed to achieve a higher level of thinking. The alternative is remaining stuck in the me-here-and-now perspective.

Seeing Clearly What We Already Know

It is telling what happened when Intel notified its customers that the company would no longer support memory chips. Wary of the reaction, the company carefully controlled when and how this communication was made. Turns out, it was a nonevent. In fact, some customers reacted with, "It sure took you a long time." As Grove admitted, "Those on the outside could see clearly what those on the inside could not."[6]

In setting their egos aside, Moore and Grove processed the decision in a way that did not pass judgment on themselves but on "someone else," a task less fraught with threat and less prone to defensiveness. They had been stuck in a low construal level until they stepped out of themselves and considered their predicament from a higher level. They could now see their situation more clearly, without their attachment to their identity as memory chip makers. They were no longer stuck wondering *how* to continue making memory chips. They could now ponder the previously unacceptable question, *Should* we be making memory chips? They were able to elevate their thinking to *what, whether,* and *why*—instantly.

The pivot to microprocessors happened when Moore and Grove each *became someone else,* their replacements. The spatial distance triggered by viewing the far-off Ferris wheel was not a coincidence. After all, Grove recalled this detail specifically twelve years later when he wrote his book. It anchored him *somewhere else* in space, helping him to psychologically distance himself. Moore and Grove then determined what was in the best interest of Intel moving forward, *sometime else*, entering a different era from their memory chip legacy.

Moore and Grove weren't the only ones facing a market shift; so was Digital Equipment Corporation (DEC). Also known simply as Digital, the company was headquartered in Maynard, Massachusetts, which bordered Concord, where David grew up. Some of his high school friends had parents who worked there. Digital was cofounded by Ken Olson in 1957, who remained president until 1992. DEC was known for minicomputers, high-quality refrigerator-size computers that were the smallest at the time that could run UNIX, a powerful programming language. That is, until the microcomputers powered by Intel microprocessors came along.

DEC missed the shift to microcomputers. Ken Olsen would have been president for more than twenty years by this point, and you could practically hear him say, DEC is minicomputers, and minicomputers is DEC! Following the market shift, Olsen was forced out of the company he had founded.[7] It's easy to see this as a failure to read the market, analyze the trends, and predict the future, but it probably had more to do with DEC becoming immersed in its own worldview and being anchored in its past decisions.

Distancing helped Gordon Moore let go and say, "Get us out of memories." We know how that worked out: As of 2024, 64 percent of desktop PCs and 75 percent of laptops have Intel microprocessors inside them.

How do we create this psychological distance? How do we get out of our own heads and improve both our decision-making and our performance in the process? Moore and Grove imagined they were their replacements. We can imagine we are any number of personas—a beloved former boss, a trusted colleague, a supportive parent, a best friend. However, over and over, we have come back to what we've found to be an extremely accessible, powerful, and effective persona: Coach.

The Distanced Self as Coach

What do all the best athletes and some of the most successful CEOs have in common?

They have coaches. Atul Gawande, famed surgeon and author of the *New York Times* bestseller *The Checklist Manifesto: How to Get Things Right*, described a coach in a *New Yorker* article this way:

> Coaches are not teachers, but they teach. They're not your boss—in professional tennis, golf, and skating, the athlete hires and fires the coach—but they can be bossy. They don't even have to be good at the sport. The famous Olympic gymnastics coach Bela Karolyi couldn't do a split if his life depended on it. Mainly, they observe, they judge, and they guide.[8]

They judge? Yes, they have to. We want our coach to be discerning and weigh in on how we are doing, how well we could be doing, and then help us close the gap. Our coach is on our side. They want what's best for us, and they apply their best objective judgment to get us on a path of continuous improvement.

But not everyone can afford to have a coach, and a coach may not always be present at the exact moment we're being called to perform, whether that means making a decision, delivering a presentation, or responding to a setback.

If being self-immersed means having a me-here-and-now perspective, then we become Coach by using self, spatial, and temporal distancing: *Be someone else. Be somewhere else. Be sometime else.* First, as Coach, we are not us. We are *someone else.* This activates psychological distance and the neutral observer perspective. Second, as Coach, we are *somewhere else.* We are physically displaced from the field of play. From the sidelines, we see ourselves as just one player in a complex environment involving many others. Third, as Coach, we can also go *sometime else.* We activate our inner time traveler. We more clearly assess past actions and future options. The focus is on what comes next.

You can become your own coach using these distancing tools. Building these habits will allow you to exit your self-immersed state while also helping others to do the same. This more adaptive perspective supports greater learning, better decision-making, improved performance, and healthier relationships because you are no longer attached to your ego and the self-serving biases and defensiveness that limit your thinking. Better yet, these techniques are free, inexhaustible, and always accessible to you. Anybody can activate this superpower. And once you do, you will see the world more clearly and live a fuller life.

PART II

Be Someone Else

3

Become Coach

For there is no such flatterer as is a man's self;
and there is no such remedy against flattery of
a man's self, as the liberty of a friend.

—SIR FRANCIS BACON

An analysis of chief executive officer (CEO) tenure and firm value based on the S&P 1500 found that, on average, CEO effectiveness peaked at fourteen years and declined from there.[1] The research firm Spencer Stuart discovered that CEOs experience their top performance in years eleven through fourteen of their tenure. Bill George, a CEO coach and Harvard Business School executive fellow, estimates that ten years is optimal. But the moment of peak effectiveness may come even earlier. A May 2024 *New York Times* article titled "The C.E.O.s Who Just Won't Quit" cited a broad-based study by Xueming Luo and colleagues, covering 356 businesses in America and China that identified 4.8 years as the ideal tenure for CEOs.[2]

Of course, there are exceptions. Warren Buffett has been CEO of Berkshire Hathaway for more than fifty years, and its stock is still going strong. Jensen Huang has been CEO of NVIDIA for the last three decades, and its stock value has skyrocketed by more than 3,000 percent over the past five years. But on the whole, the evidence suggests that most leaders lose effectiveness with time. In other words, they become part of the problem.

One reason for diminishing effectiveness is that as CEOs become entrenched, they rely more on internal networks for information; and because they have more invested in the firm, they become more loss averse, favoring decisions biased toward avoiding losses over pursuing gains. This is "playing not to lose" rather than "playing to win."

Columbia management scholars Donald Hambrick and Gregory Fukutomi explain the rise and fall of CEO effectiveness in terms of seasons.[3] For business leaders, the early seasons are characterized by an increase in effectiveness as they learn their company, gain industry knowledge, and hone their craft. In the CEO's later seasons, their work is defined by a gradual but steadily increasing commitment to their worldview, or what Hambrick and Fukutomi call the "CEO's paradigm," their understanding of how their company works within the industry to turn a profit. For Moore and Grove, the paradigm was memory chips. As Grove said, "After all, memories were us."

Hambrick and Fukutomi describe how increased commitment to the paradigm develops based on three main factors: previous investment, visibility, and longevity. First, once CEOs have made an investment in something, it's harder to change or reverse course. This is true whether it's a new product line or initiative, or a stock they have faith in to "bounce back." As the authors describe, "With the passage of time, an executive's psychological investment in his or her paradigm inexorably increases."

Second, CEOs make choices in public, visible for all to see—employees, customers, investors, peers, and competitors, among others. Their decisions are subject to judgment, question, criticism, even potential ridicule. Were they to go back on their decision or change course, they may be considered uncertain, flighty, or unstable. If they can't make up their minds, what good are they as leaders?

And finally, CEOs often consider their length of tenure as a validation of their paradigm. The longer they're in the C-suite, the more they believe their approach is correct. As Hambrick and Fukutomi point out, this makes sense since "CEOs generally are allowed to continue in their jobs only as long as their performances are satisfactory." Note that they say "satisfactory"—it's not as if their results need to be outstanding, just good enough that they don't get canned. Meanwhile, when they receive praise for their work, which they often do from the people around them, including employees, their paradigm becomes only further ingrained. Moore and Grove mitigated the longevity effect by looking at the problem as if it were their first day on the job.

HOW-TO 1: Become your replacement. Let's say you have a decision you've been grappling with. Walk out of the room. Now become someone else. Imagine you are your own replacement. Leave your tenure, your role, your attachments behind. You know little of the company and less about why things are done the way they are. You have no attachment to any particular policies or products. Settled into your new identity? Now walk back in. What would you now do differently?

CEOs are not the only people susceptible to these effects. When David was the commander of the nuclear submarine USS *Santa Fe*, he met with each crew member after they'd been there for three years. Typically, crew members are assigned a tour length of three to five years. He wanted to keep those with longer tours fresh and avoid the same kind of entrenchment that would happen to CEOs. He would send them home for the weekend with the charge that they do a reset like Grove and Moore. When they returned on Monday, he asked them to imagine that they were someone new—say, from a different submarine or from a different service even—so they saw with fresh eyes.

HOW-TO 2: Start fresh. You can try this too. The next time you go on vacation, give yourself a full reset. A week might be enough. You could also work temporarily in a different department. Some companies will deliberately rotate people in different functions to create this sense of newness or offer sabbaticals to employees so they can gain a new perspective to bring back to their craft. When you come back, deliberately return to work as if you were someone else, starting anew. Take note of your observations.

The point is to periodically detach from your existing paradigm. A core consequence of a CEO's commitment to their existing paradigm is a decrease in the diversity of information sources. In the early seasons, CEOs start out seeking a healthy dose of external information about their situation and how to respond. Typically, the share of information is balanced, with about half from external sources and half from internal sources. Then, as the CEO feels more and more certain that they've learned the ropes and the internal sources are sufficiently reliable, their curiosity about external sources dwindles and they favor their internal sources.

This results in a self-reinforcing narrowing of information. Employees who tell CEOs what they like to hear are heard more often, and CEOs hear more of what they like. This active filtering, combined with natural confirmation bias, results in a cycle where CEOs see and attend only to information that is in tune with their paradigm. Meanwhile, the less comfortable external, diverse, and dissenting information sources fall away or are filtered out. Think about the self-reinforcing story that Boeing leadership told themselves about the readiness and necessity of getting the 737 MAX to market.

In a famous fictional example from *To Kill a Mockingbird*, Judge Taylor attempts to run his court in a way that will level the playing field for the black defendant, Tom Robinson.[4] He sees the overt discrimination among the jurors and the inequity in the proceedings and admonishes his courtroom, "People generally see what they look for and hear what they listen for." At the same time, he remains blind to some of his own biases, particularly in his acceptance of the broader structures and racial prejudices of Maycomb.

In politics, long-serving autocrats harden in their positions; politicians on both sides of the aisle get trapped in their own echo chambers. This is why there is such wisdom in term limits. The longer the tenure, the more the environment of those in power begins to reflect their own self-immersed condition.

Consider the implications if our peak effectiveness in each area of our life parallels the timing shown in the CEO studies: fifteen years at most! We are all guilty of getting stuck in our own paradigms and worldviews, at work and in our personal lives. This is reinforced only by all the social media algorithms that show us more of what we have viewed in the past. The increasing comfort may make us feel better about ourselves, but it comes at the cost of distorting reality and creating webs of attachment to our previous decisions and beliefs. Our learning curve flattens, yielding few additional gains. Eventually, the negatives outweigh the positives, and our effectiveness curve starts to decline. In effect, we become detached from the truth of the situation around us. If only we could see ourselves how others see us, we'd be a lot closer to reality.

To help us get there, we need to take an alternative perspective. Call it putting on a different hat, playing a new role, or walking in someone else's shoes. There are plenty of expressions, but they all serve to help us step out of our immersed selves, see reality more clearly, understand the situation, decide our next play, and then return to ourselves to act.

When Ignorance Is Good

The Swiss Armed Forces are replacing their main combat aircraft, the F-18, with the F-35. The F-18—the older, fourth-generation airplane featured in the film *Top Gun: Maverick*—was obtained by the Swiss in an air-to-air configuration only. The F-35, however, will bring the capability for air-to-ground strikes as well as air-to-air, in addition to being a platform that is three decades more current than the F-18. These new logistical and technological capabilities were sufficient to require changes in personnel, policies, and lines of communication, resulting in a major organizational restructuring.

One of the problems the head of the Swiss Air Force, General Peter Merz, knew he would have is that people would see themselves after the reorganization as being in the same department as before the reorganization. Current weaponeers would see themselves as future weaponeers, and current logisticians would see themselves as future logisticians. Such parochialism would hinder developing the most effective organization. Reorganizations are especially challenging to execute well because they are fraught with emotion, and people are motivated to preserve power, the status quo, and one's sense of identity and community.

To circumvent these natural human tendencies, General Merz

instructed the planning team, and then the entire organization, to imagine that they did not know where or who they would be after the reorganization, in an effort to break these tribal allegiances and assumptions. This concept is called the "veil of ignorance," credited to philosopher John Rawls, who suggested thinking about the construction of societal structures and institutions from the ground up, instead of modifying existing ones. More specifically, Rawls proposed a thought experiment in which decision-makers formulating the governing principles for a just society would create these principles without knowing their identity or status—whether they were a man or a woman, rich or poor, old or young, healthy or ill, or of a specific trade or profession—in that society. Being "ignorant" in this way would render the laws impartial to any given type of person and thus for the greatest public good.

Notice how the veil of ignorance invites the same mindset as being someone else, or, in this case, being anybody else. It is a vehicle for exiting our default immersed self and seeing the situation more objectively.

HOW-TO 3: Try on the veil of ignorance. If you are responsible for a major organizational change such as a reorganization, invite the team to view the planning from the perspective of a person who has no knowledge of the existing structure and no departmental or tribal allegiances within the organization. Have them focus on the effectiveness of the organization as a whole. Perpetuate this message.

HOW-TO 4: Get an outside take. Another good time to exit your immersed self is during a performance evaluation or annual review. These situations tend to be emotional and invite people to become defensive, reducing the effectiveness of the activity and introducing resentment. If someone else were looking at what you or your team did, what would they have to say?

How We See Ourselves vs. How We See Others

Emily Pronin, a psychologist and professor at Princeton, has made a career of studying the information asymmetry between how we see ourselves and how we see others, including the conflict and disagreement that result from this perceptual gap.[5] Information asymmetry means we know different things about others than we do about ourselves. We judge ourselves based on our intentions, which we know but they do not, and we judge others based on their behaviors, which we can see clearly but they cannot. Our view of them is external, visual, but limited in understanding of their internal feelings, motivations, and intentions.

For example, if we leave the house four minutes late and hit every red light on the way to the office, when we get there we may mutter, "The traffic was bad today." It wasn't our fault, right? It was the external environment's fault—traffic or stoplights, or a favorite refrain heard in New York City: "The trains were running late." *We* weren't late. It was the trains. But when someone we are having a meeting with the next day arrives late, we may quickly think they are undisciplined, lack commitment, or did not have the foresight to use their alarm clock properly. We blame them as people, judging their shortcomings. And while we readily impugn their character, we credit their success to factors outside their control. At the same time, we externalize our own shortcomings and credit our wins to our character. Our overly charitable self-attributions form the core of our self-serving biases. We paint a rosy portrait of ourselves but not of others.

Our view of ourselves is generally scant on external, visual information and richly informed by our own feelings, motivations, and intentions. We are also less aware of how we appear based on our behaviors and actions. It's a question of being extrospective versus introspective. Whereas how we see ourselves is generally more flattering than how we see others, the difference is not fully explained by our overall self-serving bias but also reflects a literal difference in the information we have about ourselves versus others.

This difference is elegantly illustrated through a classic tool called the Johari Window. Named after the two psychologists who developed it (Joseph Luft and Harrington Ingham), the Johari Window is a 2 x 2 table that crosses (A) what I know about myself and (B) what I don't know about myself, with (1) what others know about me and (2) what others don't know about me. One cell of this table is of particular interest: the blind spot (B1). These are things that I don't know about myself but that others know about me.

	A. Known to me	B. Not known to me
1. Known to others	Open	Blind Spot
2. Not known to others	Hidden	Unknown

Another example of how we naturally process information from our self-immersed perspective comes from a classic experiment about claiming credit. When researchers ask married partners separately, "What percentage of the household chores do you do?" it may come as no surprise that, when added together, the couple's responses total more than 100 percent—typically about 130 percent.[6] The same results are found with teams at work, and the more people in the group, the higher the total percentage. On any team, we are biased to think that we have contributed more to the outcome than we actually have.

Why do we overclaim credit? Well, it is not because we are credit-hogging jerks (at least not most of us). The reason is more benign: We simply see what we do and not what others do. Known as the availability heuristic, we use readily available information to make decisions, neglecting the quality or completeness of the information. That's why when researchers ask about contributions to something negative, like arguments, the same result occurs as with the chores and team contributions: The sum is still greater than 100 percent.

It gets worse. For one, we remember discriminately. Our brains choose to encode information that conforms to our self-image as a contributing member to a relationship or team, an instance of the self-serving bias in action. And two, we retrieve the information in a selective way, more readily recalling that which supports our self-image and makes us look good. The resulting overly charitable recollection of our own contributions is a result of the immersed perspective, being stuck in our own heads, experiencing the world from behind our own eyeballs. We see the world from the me-here-and-now. So, even though we might see the dishwasher full at one point and see it empty later, this may not trigger the same sense that someone else emptied the dishwasher, compared to actually seeing them empty the dishwasher.

One method the researchers of the original overclaiming study found to mitigate our biased recollection of our own contributions is to prime people to think first of something their partner (or coworker) did before estimating their own contribution. Beginning by thinking from the other person's perspective helps people exit their immersed state in a small way, thereby enabling them to see their own contributions more accurately.

HOW-TO 5: Consider the contribution of others first. So, the next time you're concerned about how much you've contributed to developing a proposal, delivering a project, or cleaning the house, first, take the perspective of the other person and consider what they did to contribute. Then proceed to estimate your own contribution.

Let's imagine Captain Lee somehow rescued the landing and got the plane down safely. How would he remember his contribution? He would readily think of the key decisions and actions he took: pulling up on the stick at one point and noticing the engines at idle at another point. He would know, if prompted perhaps, that others made comments that reminded, helped, or expanded his view of the landing, but he would not dwell on them. Pretty soon those comments would be forgotten, and all he would be left with is evidence of his contribution.

Overestimation of our talents or knowledge and underestimation of others' leads to a slew of issues. For example, we overestimate our chances of success and underestimate the chances of others in risky projects, like starting a new business. We also overestimate how much we know someone from a brief interaction but underestimate how well someone knows us.

Information asymmetry leads us to believe our decisions are right simply because we have the free will and detachment to choose them, relying on a significant amount of personal sovereignty, an ability to think for ourselves. But we believe we can easily perceive when others have been manipulated into making certain decisions, often for social conformity. We are independent agents. Everyone else? Sheep.

Fundamentally, we rely on a host of biases and distortions that help us see ourselves as more benevolent and internally consistent than we really are. In his classic book *How to Win Friends and Influence People*, Dale Carnegie opens by hammering on the point that we don't see ourselves objectively. The worst criminals assert they are good people. Even after killing police officers and innocent civilians, these criminals claim to be well intentioned and merely misunderstood humans. We readily believe our own self-assuaging inner dialogue. But taking an observer's view—being someone else—allows us to recognize the stark disconnect between the story we tell ourselves and the one everyone else is reading.

Our brains naturally tell us that the view we have of ourselves is correct. We seek confirming evidence to validate this perspective. I see myself as loving, caring, empathetic, honest, athletic, healthy, innovative, creative, and so on.

HOW-TO 6: Ask for the evidence. Pick one of your committed self-views. Now imagine you are someone else who has the opportunity to observe your behavior frequently. Then, as this person, ask, "What is the evidence that image is true?" and "What is the evidence that image is not true?"

This practice reveals the uncomfortable, hard reality of how you really behave stripped of the knowledge of your wonderful intentions. It works because the someone else you become will not ignore your shortcomings just because you meant well.

HOW-TO 7: Yellow-card me! When you want to get better at something or change your behavior, your internal dialogue will try to convince you that you've already done so. You tell yourself that you have broken the old habit and are already doing the new one. But it's a deception. One way to avoid this self-deceiving ruse is to invite other people to "yellow-card" you. They can physically hold up a yellow card (like in soccer), they can give you a ticket (like from a roll of raffle tickets), or to really help you take the point, they can fine you a nominal amount (like ten dollars). Choose people you can openly share your goals with, who are on your side and supportive but not afraid of telling you what you might not want to hear. The behavior could be something like listening fully or recognizing a job well done, anything that you genuinely want to work on.

While people are often reluctant to yellow-card a friend, peer, or boss, once you explain that you need their help, they are more likely to agree. Start small and pick just one observable thing. Use the other person's ability to see us from the outside. They won't know why we did not listen. They will simply see that we did not do so, say, because we looked at our phone during the conversation or interrupted before they had finished speaking. If you're anything like us, your first reaction to being carded will probably be to say, "I was just . . ." The fact is that we all feel justified in these actions until we're forced to see them through someone else's eyes.

In our self-immersed states, the blind spots and the hidden areas grow. These are points of disconnection from reality. We lose awareness that we know things about ourselves, like our intention to be on time, that others do not, and we use that to excuse our own behavior. A recent study illustrated this asymmetry of awareness with "phubbing"—when someone snubs us (or we snub someone) by looking at their cell phone during a conversation. When we are talking to someone in person and they pick up their phone to answer a text or start scrolling, it's easy to get annoyed and feel that they're not really listening to what we're saying. It's devaluing. We think of them as rude, maybe self-centered, and our satisfaction with the conversation decreases.

Yet, when we feel the need to check our own phone while in a conversation with someone else, we easily justify the behavior to ourselves, even though when done to us, it dampens the interaction. We attribute our action to our positive intentions, and we overestimate our ability to multitask.[7] Note that the error is, again, asymmetric. There is more error in interpreting the effects of our own behavior, while our interpretation of the impact of the behavior of others is often more accurate—especially if we're merely a neutral observer. Imagine watching a video of yourself in a conversation. You're shocked by the number of times you check your phone, but now you know the truth. You've exited the immersed self and are able to see yourself as someone else, without distortion.

Personas

Often, we can remove our blind spot simply by taking the perspective of someone else. One thing Mike has noticed while teaching is that students would miss some key parts of an assignment. It was as if they had spent all their time writing the paper but none evaluating it against the objectives. He tried something new that would require them to become "him" prior to submitting their assignment. Instead of merely providing them with the grading rubric, which they were apparently free to ignore before, he required everyone to grade their own paper using the rubric. This forced them to exit their self-immersed perspective and instead become a distanced evaluator.

This worked surprisingly well. First, the papers were better, and fewer students totally missed portions of the rubric. Second, this approach provided a more fundamental learning opportunity than merely writing a paper. If the student's grades were close to his own read of the paper, he let their grade stand, reinforcing not only the writing exercise but also the distanced self-evaluation exercise.

HOW-TO 8: Create the rubric for yourself. Before diving into a project or activity, imagine yourself as Coach and be clear about what you are trying to achieve. How would you know you met your goals? Write them down. Create your own grading criteria. Then set that aside and go to work. At the end, step out of the work and look back at Coach's previously determined goals and evaluate Mike's work.

When we put on the hat of someone else—for example, a trusted peer, an objective evaluator, or a benevolent coach—we become someone else. This imbues us with clarity of perspective. But it can also be a boon to performance or persistence.

Beyoncé is one of the most popular musical artists of all time. She is bold and confident, right? Well, she has said otherwise. As Beyoncé explained to Oprah, "I could never walk out here and do that."[8] In order to become the phenomenal performer she wanted to be, Beyoncé created an alter ego who is fearless, brash, and glamorous. Before she goes onstage, Beyoncé becomes someone else. She transforms into Sasha Fierce and delivers a knockout performance. It's a temporary state because when the performance is over, the "true" Beyoncé emerges again.

Alter egos like Sasha Fierce are not uncommon. They are often created for the purpose of improving performance. When we become our alter egos, we leave our old bodies, our insecurities, and our fears behind. We become a different person.

Becoming someone else also improves the persistence of on-task behavior. Setting aside the superpowers that accompany most on-screen alter egos, a multi-university research team tested what is known as the "Batman Effect": improved perseverance by impersonating an exemplary other person.[9] Four- and six-year-old children were brought into a lab to complete a task on a laptop. Whenever they saw a piece of cheese on the screen, they were supposed to press the space bar. They were instructed to do nothing if they saw a cat. The task was purposefully long and boring, but the kids were told it was important and that their hard work was helpful.

The 180 kids were randomly assigned to one of three conditions. In the first, they were told to think about their *own* feelings and to ask themselves, "Am *I* working hard?" In the second, they were supposed to use their *own name* and to ask themselves, "Is [*name*] working hard?" In the third, they needed to think about someone else who is a hard worker—such as Batman—and to ask themselves, "Is Batman working hard?" To drive home the point for group three, they were also given a cape.

Sure enough, those in the Batman group persisted the longest, followed by the [*name*] group, with those in the self-immersed group persisting the least. Naturally, the six-year-olds generally persisted longer than the four-year-olds, but the four-year-olds in the Batman group actually worked as long as the six-year-olds in the immersed group! When kids *became* Batman, they worked the hardest.

When we imagine ourselves as someone else, we access the strengths of that alter ego and break out of any self-consciousness and attachments to our prior decisions. But in order to apply this effect to our everyday life, we need to capture this perspective and carry it into our day-to-day reality or, at the very least, to the decision we're currently facing.

It's simple enough to say "be someone else" or become Coach, but it helps to have a concrete idea of who we become to be "not me."

In a Foreign Language

Becoming someone else—Coach, for example—works because as we exit our immersed selves, we drop the baggage of our prior decisions, preconceptions, and ideas of who we are as a person. It is even possible to partly neutralize deeply held beliefs from our sociocultural background.

Eye-opening evidence of the ability to shed our experience-based biases comes from research studying the effects of decision-making while thinking about the problem in a foreign language. In a study aptly titled "Piensa Twice," Albert Costa and colleagues gave bilingual English- and Spanish-speaking people decision-making tasks either in English or Spanish.[10] Some were native English speakers, and some were native Spanish speakers.

The focus of the study was on a specific decision-making bias, loss aversion, which causes us to value things we *own* more than those we don't. For example, it hurts more to lose twenty dollars we had than it pleases us to find a twenty-dollar bill. This bias is the source of multiple distortions in our decision-making, from escalation of commitment to quitting too late. It even influences when we choose to start receiving Social Security payments. The study found that the otherwise ubiquitous effects of loss aversion were mitigated when people thought about the problem in a non-native language.

A study on pain perception shows a similar effect of stripping out our socio-emotional wiring. When people reported pain in their native language, they perceived it more strongly than when in their nonnative language. We surmise that this is for the same reason loss aversion is mitigated: There is a separation that occurs from our true and fully immersed self when we switch to a nonnative language, even if we are fluent in it.[11]

Who Is Coach?

Before Kahneman passed away, former professional poker player Annie Duke, who now writes about cognitive behavior and decision-making, spoke with him about the secret behind the crucial decision of when to quit—the subject of her bestselling book *Quit*. He told her, "What everybody needs is the friend who really loves them but does not care much about hurt feelings in the moment."[12] The beauty of this recommendation is that we actually have the capability to be that person ourselves.

How many times have you seen an obvious problem a close friend or family member seemed blind to? Well, you should know that for every time you have, one of your close friends or relatives saw an obvious problem in your behavior you were blind to as well. Take child-rearing: It is a lot easier to raise other people's kids! When your children act out in public, it's just another day in your life as a parent; when someone else's does, you wonder why they insist on encouraging such bad behavior. We are more likely to see the problems in other people's actions and decisions than our own.

A commonly cited example of this blindness is found in the story of ancient Israel's King Solomon. Nobility from around the known world would travel to seek his counsel, and he dispensed wisdom in return—but only when it came to the affairs of others.

He was a poor parent, whose sons turned into tyrants; he had many mistresses; and he lived with shortsighted extravagance. By the end of his life, he had become a greedy king, no better than any others who are still lambasted centuries later. This legacy gave rise to what's referred to as "Solomon's paradox"—great wisdom when it comes to the affairs of others, but foolishness when it comes to one's own decisions.[13]

Becoming Coach can help us avoid this cruel fate, as it allows us to appraise any situation from a distance. Coach is an independent observer. Someone separate from you who sees you matter-of-factly, as you are. Coach has your best interests at heart. Coach is realistic yet supportive and encouraging. Coach sees your mistakes and poor excuses without judgment, and values progress over perfection.

Who is Coach for you? A mother figure or father figure? A positive amalgamation of beloved, trusted people in your life? What qualities or attributes does Coach have? What does Coach look like?

Coach does not need to be a specific real person or persons but sure could be inspired by one. Some favorites might be Nelson Mandela, Oprah Winfrey, Bill Belichick, Buddha, Chuck Norris, Dolly Parton, Dale Carnegie, Malala Yousafzai, Gandhi, Jesus, Michelle Obama, John Wayne, John Wooden, Mother Teresa, Muhammad, Peter Drucker, Melinda Gates, Phil Jackson, Steven Spielberg, Tony Dungy, and Warren Buffett. They could also be fictitious: Yoda, Katniss Everdeen, Robin Hood, Black Panther, Jo March, Supergirl, and Jack Reacher.

The point is that Coach isn't you. So, *anyone* who is *not you* is an improvement. And Coach does not need to be the same in all situations. Maybe you become Suze Orman for a financial decision or Judge Judy to arbitrate a sibling dispute.

When we return to ourselves, we leave that image of Coach "out there," still observing us with the same impartiality. We can use this image of Coach for accountability. We want to follow the plan and make Coach proud. If our motivation lags, Coach encourages us: "C'mon, you can do it!" By becoming Coach, we help ourselves in a way we couldn't otherwise.

HOW-TO 9: Choose the form Coach takes. Think of a decision you are facing. For this specific situation, choose who you want to become as Coach. Mentally inhabit that persona. What does Coach see? What questions does Coach have? What would Coach advise? What would Coach say is the most important thing to focus on? Write down the answers to all these questions. Then return to yourself and execute.

Or in the case of a performance, to gain the needed perspective and composure for the task at hand, become your alter ego.

To be clear, we are not advocating that you live your life as Coach or as anyone else, for that matter. We do not recommend inhabiting your alter ego for any considerable period of time. Our prescription is for you to become someone else temporarily to gain the distance, perspective, and clarity necessary to make a big decision. Then go back to being yourself and execute on that decision, with the increased perspective afforded by Coach's distance.

How to Become Coach

1. **Become your replacement.** When you have a decision to make, imagine you are your replacement, like Moore and Grove did.

2. **Start fresh.** After a vacation, work anniversary, or period away from your current position, return to work with fresh eyes.

3. **Try on the veil of ignorance.** For an organizational change effort, apply a veil of ignorance—for you and for your team.

4. **Get an outside take.** During a review, consider what a team looking at your team's performance would take away from it.

5. **Consider the contribution of others first.** View the other person's contributions from their perspective before estimating your own contribution.

6. **Ask for the evidence.** Become someone else and objectively consider the evidence that your self-beliefs are true.

7. **Yellow-card me!** When you want feedback on your own behavior or are trying to change a habit, invite someone you trust to yellow-card you.

8. **Create the rubric for yourself.** Become Coach to create the rubric for your own task. Apply the rubric.

9. **Choose the form Coach takes.** Exit yourself and inhabit this form. Make the decision from Coach's perspective, and then return to yourself to execute.

Summary

The point of becoming Coach is not to stop listening to any other coaches or mentors you may already have in your life. Instead, it's to recognize that, more often than not, *you* have the answers to the big questions inside you already. You just can't see them because you are too self-immersed. It's like you're looking through the periscope in one direction on high power mode, while the answers lie in another. Coach ensures you've got the right sight. Coach is supportive. Coach has a plan. Not just a tactical plan but a strategic plan. Coach remains calm, collected, and supportive when you get discouraged, agitated, or angry, when you're prone to doing something self-destructive, or when you're just not living up to your best self.

4

Talk Like Coach

Simone, chill. Sit down. We're not doing it.

—SIMONE BILES, ON QUITTING
THE 2020 OLYMPICS

Ethan Kross was born and raised in Brooklyn, New York, where he grew up in Canarsie, a working-class neighborhood in the southeastern part of the borough. Today, he's a professor in the University of Michigan's top-ranked psychology department and the Ross School of Business, as well as the director of the Emotion and Self-Control Laboratory, which he founded in 2008. In his book *Chatter*, Kross recalls that when he was a child, his father would habitually tell him that whenever he had a problem he should: "Ask yourself the question."[1] Young Ethan gave it a try, and in time, he began developing a rapport with himself.

As Kross got older, he became more interested in these inner conversations about the decisions he had to make as a teenager— about social interactions, for example, or plans for college. He began to trust that voice within as it guided him sagely through those years. A degree in psychology seemed only natural. While Kross's deliberate introspection would often lead to wise, beneficial choices and positive emotions, he learned from his psychology classes that this was not always the case for many. More often than not, when people spoke to themselves, they tended to dwell on past injustices, stoking negative emotions and magnifying distress. The result was emotional fragility, compromised decisions, damaged relationships, and undermined performance.

Kross wanted to understand the differing results. What distinguishes positive introspection from unhelpful rumination? The answer became clear: People who were able to escape self-immersion and achieve a distanced state felt better, performed better, decided better, and lived better than those who were stuck in their past. He noticed that some people who achieved positive introspection had referred to themselves in the third person, as if they were someone else. There is a word for this: *illeism*. For example, instead of "I have to make a decision," it was "David has to make a decision" or "He has to make a decision." Illeism, a form of distanced self-talk, seemed to be an effective way for people to create psychological distance.

Once Kross recognized the potential benefits of illeism, he and his colleagues wanted to know just how helpful it would be to deliberately reframe our internal chatter from the first person to the third person to nudge us into that distanced state.[2] In these studies, participants were placed in some kind of stressful situation. They could be asked to simply consider a distressing event from the past, or they experienced a laboratory-induced stressor. Some were instructed to reflect on the stressor from an immersed, first-person perspective, while others were asked to take a distanced, third-person perspective.

In one study, students were tasked to deliver a speech about their qualifications for their dream job to a panel of trained interviewers. They were given only five minutes to prepare and were not allowed to take notes. In psychological experiments, unprepared public speaking is a surefire way to induce stress in participants. Stress biases us toward a more immersed, me-here-and-now experience of the world that is hyperaware of threats, real and perceived. It activates fear and anxiety. The self-immersed students were told to use *I* in a self-reflection to prepare for the interview, while the distanced half used illeism: *he, she,* or their name. Those in the illeism group reported less anxiety, shame, and rumination, and their speeches scored higher than those of the first-person participants.

In another study, undergraduate women were told they would have a conversation with a male participant with the goal of making a good first impression and that the conversation would be video recorded and assessed by a trained psychologist who would rate their social skills. Half were asked to think about the experience using the pronouns *I* and *my* as much as possible, while the other half were instructed to use their own name or *you* instead. Then they were introduced to their male partners and observed. Again, results showed that those in the distanced group utilizing illeism performed better and had lower levels of anxiety after the interaction.

Kross's research found that most of us rarely take advantage of illeism to activate this distanced approach, particularly when reflecting on a previous event, especially an unpleasant one. We tend to *relive* (Kross uses *recount*) the experience from the first-person, self-immersed perspective over and over again. This results in re-experiencing stress on repeat, digging that mental rut even further, and reducing the likelihood of seeing the event in a new light. There are negative long-term consequences of this continued rehashing, such as greater susceptibility to emotional hijacking, vulnerability to recurring negative thoughts, and increased rumination.

Kross's subjects who employed illeism experienced a narrative reinterpretation of an event rather than simply reliving it. For those who suffered from depression, the more severe their symptoms, the more illeism helped. Given that the 2023 National Survey of Children's Health reported 8.4 percent of adolescents had been diagnosed with depression, up from 5.8 percent in 2016, this is a strikingly useful finding.[3]

To connect this to construal level theory, illeism allows people to "reconstrue" the event. This is a powerful reframe, allowing people to see the event afresh, with a more balanced perspective, lowering their stress, and reducing their susceptibility to emotional hijacking.[4]

Distanced Self-Talk

This simple linguistic exercise is one of the easiest ways to exit the immersed me-here-and-now perspective. Replace the singular first-person pronouns we use to describe ourselves, *I*, *me*, and *my*, with the third person: for example, your name, *he*, *she*, or *they*. It works because when we write or talk about ourselves as if we were someone else, we feel like we are someone else.

We love illeism. It's as close to a free lunch as we've found. This approach is easy to do, it can be applied in many situations, and most people report that when talking about or writing about themselves in the second or third person, they immediately feel different. We're not the only fans of this approach. When Jennifer Lawrence got flustered during an interview and wanted a reset, the actress used illeism: "OK, get ahold of yourself, Jennifer."[5]

Similarly, Anne Hathaway provides a rich case study of the process and benefits for exiting the immersed self, taking on a distanced perspective, and reengaging. In an interview she gave the Associated Press in 2012 about the film adaptation of the musical

Les Misérables, the actress described how she was already feeling self-conscious, having just recently buzzed her hair short before she was to sing the iconic "I Dreamed a Dream."[6] The pressure was on, and she had worked up the courage. But once she faced the cameras, she became anxious again, realizing that once the film came out, it "was going to be forever." She was focused on how exposed she would feel if she messed up. Unsatisfied with her first takes, she called a time-out. She tells it like this:

> "No, no. Stop. I'm sorry. The balance, it's off." And that's when I took the earpieces and stuck them in my ears. I closed my eyes and I remember thinking, "Hathaway, if you do not do this in this moment, you have no right to call yourself an actor. Put aside all that bulls— and just do your job." I opened my eyes and I'm like [snaps fingers]: "Let's go." And I did it. That was the one that I let rip and that was the one that was in the piece.

Hathaway uses the power of distanced self-talk to achieve the reframe and refocus she needed. Notice how she's herself, immersed in performance, and stressed. She exits self-immersion by talking to herself in the third person, as if she were her own coach. Then she reenters the here and now and performs.

When the most decorated American gymnast in history, Simone Biles, made the gut-wrenching decision to pull out of the 2020 Tokyo Olympics, she told herself, "Simone, chill. Sit down. We're not doing it."[7] She knew she wasn't in the mental space to perform at her best, and she took this distanced perspective to convince herself of what she knew, deep down, to be true.

We've all probably done this in a stressful situation at one point or another to psyche ourselves up. Before we're about to give a presentation or speech, we encourage ourselves with a *You can do it*, echoing a coach, teacher, or parent, perhaps. Day to day, however, we tend to use *I* more, especially when talking about our feelings.[8] The problem is that *I* serves to cement us in our default immersed state, especially when we are struggling. When our executive function is already under duress, this *I*-focused rumination and catastrophizing is unhelpful. Such rumination results in changes to the neural circuitry associated with our sense of self, internalizing negative feedback and impairing our reaction time, executive functioning, and attentional control.[9]

Thinking, speaking, and writing about ourselves in the second or third person creates an automatic distancing, a self-reflection that we would otherwise be less likely to access. It nudges us toward viewing ourselves as *other*, and we can't help but step out of our immersed self. Indeed, Biles's decision to sit out the Tokyo games, brutal as it must have been to make, was a wise one. She saved herself from the probability of serious injury, and her example made it OK for other athletes to speak up when they knew something was off and to talk openly about prioritizing their mental health.

Biles returned to competition at the USA Classic in 2023, winning her events handily. She then competed in the 2023 World Artistic Gymnastics Championships in Antwerp, Belgium. She wasn't even that concerned about the outcome. "As long as I'm out there twisting again, having and finding the joy for gymnastics again, who cares?"[10] She proceeded to win four gold medals at the event. She continued that streak at the 2024 Olympics in Paris, where she won three gold medals, for all-around, team, and women's vault (the Yurchenko double pike, her signature move and the most difficult vault to pull off, sealed the result).

With a grand total of eleven Olympic medals (seven gold, two silver, and two bronze) and thirty World Championship medals,

Simone Biles is the most decorated gymnast in history and is widely hailed as the greatest of all time.

Like Biles, we can all use illeism to help us exit our self-immersed state and achieve the perspective that comes from psychological distance to make the right decisions that will serve us best in the long term.

Jen Pierce left a fast-paced career leading commodity traders to coach executives. In an interview with us, she described her experience using illeism with herself and her clients:

> When I talk to myself in the third person, it's much easier for me to realize I'm being an emotional wreck. When I'm just like, oh my God, everybody hates me. I did this. Instead, I say OK, let's be the observer. I'm now managing me. I'm the director. I'm looking at this employee who happens to be me. That, for me, is what being the observer is. That's what I teach clients. It's not like it's some big pie in the sky thing. Just pretend you're talking to yourself in third person. "Wait, Jennifer's really acting emotional right now. I wonder if this is a good decision for her to respond like this."

In the interest of protecting whatever sanity may still exist in the world, we wish to offer an important clarification, lest overzealous readers draw the wrong conclusion about how to use this mental tool. Lawrence, Hathaway, Biles, and Pierce are all relaying personal internal dialogues they had *with themselves*. We are *not* advocating that everyone run around talking about themselves to others in the third person. (That would be strange. And really annoying.) Distanced self-talk is a strategy you should use for just that—*self*-talk—which will help you coach yourself to better outcomes.

Better Performance, Less Anxiety

The power of illeism is clear. High achievers across domains have found that it leads to better performance, and years of research by Ethan Kross and others have shown that using distanced self-talk helps with the following:

▶ Higher-level thinking

▶ Decreased anxiety and shame

▶ Shift in view of future stressors as challenges as opposed to threats

▶ Improved first impressions and public speaking

▶ Reduced post-event rumination

HOW-TO 1: Hey, [your name]. As you muse over a tough decision, reflect on the situation using your own name. You'll notice that something immediately changes. When you talk to yourself using your own name, it's like the person talking automatically becomes *not you*, freeing you from any mental and emotional baggage. Illeism showcases the simple yet incredible power of language—verbal or written—to help us reframe a situation with the advantage of a clearer and elevated perspective.

An example many of us can relate to is trying to make healthy food choices. Every day, we are confronted over and over again with a choice between a healthy option or a tasty but not so healthy option. It happens every time we prepare a meal, get a snack, or feel hungry. Over the course of a day, these decisions can wear down our self-control to the point where we give in.

When questioning your every decision about what to eat,

something as simple as what's for breakfast can become a moment of stress—whether you should have that extra piece of buttered toast, skip the bacon, have an orange instead of orange juice, avoid carbs altogether, drink a fruit smoothie, or maybe not have breakfast at all. You might even start to dread mealtimes, anticipating the anxiety that is likely to bubble up. But studies show that psychological distancing through illeism, or the use of the third-person perspective, actually helps you make healthier food choices throughout the day.

Distancing makes it easier to access your more abstract, higher-order goals, like the kind of person you really want to be, or some longer-term goals like getting in shape or competing in a triathlon. In other words, distanced self-talk encourages us to consider our lives more fully. Next time you go to the pantry or fridge, instead of asking yourself, Hmmm, what do I want to eat? try, What does [your name] want to eat? If you're aiming to eat better, you'll recognize a pull toward a healthier decision. In all fairness, some of us may eat whatever we want, without any concerns of long-term health effects. In fact, dieters tend to feel ambivalent about their food choices, being acutely torn between tastier treats and healthier options, as either cause or consequence of them being on a diet.

This is why, in a study by Kross and colleagues on dieting and distanced self-talk, it was necessary first to prime participants with a two-minute video on the importance of being healthy and active.[11] This pairing of health-related information with self-distancing led to healthier choices. So, though distanced self-talk helps you make better food choices, you must first be honest: What does [your name] really want from their life? If it's to eat whatever you want whenever you want, but you recognize the need for a healthier diet, you may need a subtle reminder of your health goals every now and then before you take the third-person approach. For example, you could tape a note on the refrigerator, REMEMBERING THEIR HEALTH GOALS, WHAT WOULD [YOUR NAME] WANT TO EAT? and then make a choice.

This works because distanced self-talk activates higher levels of construal, which connect with greater meaning and purpose and hence create more stability over time. Consider this contrast: In the self-immersed perspective, you might say, "I eat heathy by eliminating sugar." The self-distanced perspective leads you to a higher level of construal, so after self-distancing, you might return to the first-person perspective and say, "I live a fuller, more active life by eating healthy." Notice that in the self-immersed frame, you connect eating healthy with a lower-level, more detailed action; whereas in the self-distanced frame, eating healthy follows from a greater purpose. This reframe helps you more naturally want to act out the concrete details that align with your bigger *why*. This is why David makes better decisions about eating than *I* do.

In general, healthy habits are hard to develop on your own. But as you use the third-person approach, you are talking to yourself in words that Coach would use to talk to you. You have an ally in Coach. Let's say you want to start going to the gym on the way home from work. According to Katy Milkman, a professor at Wharton and author of a study on habit formation, incorporating a new habit like that will take four to seven months.[12] Something simpler, like eating a piece of fruit at lunch, took an average of sixty-six days based on another study.[13] Either way, you need to keep at it and not get derailed during the fragile period of burning it into muscle memory.

HOW-TO 2: Coach makes the call. As Coach, make the choice about what to eat once or about going to the gym just once. If you re-contemplate the decision to drive to the gym after work or at each turn on the way home, you'll end up skipping the gym because it takes only one of those multiple opportunities to send you home. Outsource the decision to Coach and stick to it. Coach (you, as Coach) writes the plan. Later, you (as yourself) execute it. You can even write the plan in advance. In the case of a workout routine, if you commit to just following the plan, no further decisions are required.

A bit of time separation helps, too, such as writing the plan the day before a workout. If you just jump into the day without Coach's plan, it's too easy to get stuck in the me-here-and-now perspective, and you're likely to get offtrack.

The Body Knows

When we are self-immersed, it is easy to become self-righteous. We can even feel this on a visceral level.

> At the point when I realized that my rather silly statement—"Do you know who I am?"—wasn't going to work, I should have shut up and let it go. But I didn't. Unfortunately, instead of restraint and a little humility, it was righteous indignation that ran through my veins.[14]

Sarasota (where we live) politician Martin Hyde is unapologetically aggressive when challenged in the political arena. Effective? Maybe. But his egotistical confrontational behavior sure did backfire on him during a simple traffic stop.

Hyde was stopped for going 57 mph in a 40 mph zone in his jet-black Range Rover. He was seen texting at the same time. Body-cam footage shows Hyde asking the officer if she knew who he was within thirty seconds of their interaction.[15] "You know who I am, right?" It is painful to watch.

He proceeded by threatening the officer's job, dismissing what she had to say, and refusing to provide registration. The officer stayed on task, replying, "Still have a job to do, sir." Hyde replied by defending his character—"I'm a law-abiding citizen"—and attacking her motivations: "You think you're being witty?" . . . "Why are you lying? . . . You knew exactly what you were doing when you made this stop." Then, to a different officer, he said: "We're going to make sure she pays the price for being disrespectful. . . . I know exactly who she is." From watching the footage, it is clear that the officer who made the stop was *not* the person being disrespectful during this encounter.

Following the social media fallout and "hundreds of calls," Hyde offered something of an apology in the local paper.[16] It had the sort of spin one would expect from a politician: "People like someone to stand behind and—both in terms of girth and character—I'm one of those people who people with a beef like to have on their side." But it also does an excellent job of laying out in plain English how it *feels* when we become locked in the me-here-and-now self: "It was righteous indignation that ran through my veins." We could all stand to take this visceral feeling as a big, bright warning sign that we are dangerously self-immersed.

Self-distancing has beneficial effects on the physiological level. In a study conducted by social psychologist Lindsey Streamer and colleagues,[17] participants prepared and then delivered a speech to a selection board on why they were qualified for their dream job. They were primed for the immersed- or distanced-self state by writing the speech using either first- or third-person pronouns. They delivered the speech while hooked up to an electrocardiogram (ECG) machine that monitored their cardiovascular system response.

The cardiovascular system of the immersed-self group looked like it was responding to a threat. How does it feel to be threatened? We're on high alert, our vision narrows, and our adrenaline kicks in. It's scary. Portions of our cardiovascular system constrict, pushing blood back toward our heart, getting the body ready for fight or flight.

In contrast, the cardiovascular system of the distanced-self group looked like it was responding to a *challenge*. Now, how does it feel to rise to a challenge? It's expansive. We are curious, eager, seeking. We widen our aperture and become more aware of what's around us. It's fun. There's a chance of winning, as compared to just "not losing."

These effects have impressive endurance. The researchers found that these trends carried over into the participant's next speech on a totally unrelated topic. That means the effect is robust enough to influence other tasks once we've finished the current one.

HOW-TO 3: Get psyched. Prepare for a stressful event using illeism. Write it out or say it in your head. Allow the distanced perspective to offer you a sense of calm. That person you're talking about now has an opportunity to rise to the challenge. It is not threatening; it is an exciting opportunity.

Distanced self-talk also helps reduce stress because it removes some of the emotional baggage that tends to cloud thinking, decreasing performance. A study led by Jason Moser at Michigan State University tested this idea by hooking participants up to a functional magnetic resonance imaging (fMRI) machine to measure event-related potentials (ERPs), brain signals that show the response of our brains to specific inputs or events.[18] Participants were then shown unpleasant, or highly aversive, images. Moser found that when people used distanced self-talk, their emotional reactivity was reduced by about half, without increasing signals of cognitive control. In other words, distanced self-talk made them less emotionally reactive, without extra effort.

Cut Through the BS

A study published in 2021 by Igor Grossmann of the University of Waterloo studied the effect of journaling, using illeism, on the ability to gain perspective and wisdom.[19] The participants were divided equally into a distanced group and an immersed group. Those in the distanced group were directed as follows: "Please describe your stream of thoughts about today's social event from a third-person perspective in detail below. To help you take the third-person perspective, use your name as much as possible as you describe the event and your stream of thoughts. For example, if your name were Chris, you might write, 'Chris thinks . . . Chris feels . . . '" Those in the immersed group were instructed this way: "Please describe your stream of thoughts about today's social event from a first-person perspective in detail below. To help you take the first-person perspective, use the pronouns *I/me* as much as possible as you describe the event and your stream of thoughts. For example, you might write, 'I think . . . I feel . . . '"

Evaluators scored the journal entries for intellectual humility, open-mindedness, recognition of diverse perspectives, and openness to compromise in conflict resolution. Collectively, psychologists call these attributes "wise reasoning," and they are linked to our sense of well-being and life satisfaction. At the end of a four-week period, those using their name demonstrated an increase in wise reasoning compared to the previous four weeks, whereas those in the immersed first-person group showed no change. This is further proof that illeism can help us across a range of functions in our life. The research is definitive on this topic, but we also recognize the strength of illeism, particularly in journaling, because we've tried it. We know others who have as well.

When David attended a swim camp in the Maldives, they talked about distanced-self language. When assessing that week's class and considering what could be done differently for the next group, swim coach Brenton Ford, who conducts these types of camps around the world, explained how he used illeism:

> I wrote in third person about how I thought last week went and what I could have improved on. The biggest difference taking this approach was I went deeper into the analysis of it because I felt like I was critiquing someone else, so I was more objective so the critique was much more honest. Reading back what I wrote on the performance, I don't feel bad that there were things I could have done better, but rather I'm excited to make some changes for this next week.

Mike tried this with his students. He had them practice journaling in the third person for some of his classes. After some initial awkwardness, the assignment got a thumbs-up all around, as the students experienced the benefits that this distanced approach created. They were coaching themselves with clarity, fewer emotional responses, and greater objectivity. Here's what some of them had to say:

▶ "It helps cut through the BS because we lie to ourselves."

▶ "It lets us hold ourselves more accountable, like, 'Do you really believe that?'"

▶ "Lets me see difficult things like it's not that big of a deal."

▶ "Can see myself with compassion."

▶ "Can see myself more truthfully."

With more practice, they found it easier to self-distance and enter the observer's perspective. It's worth building this habit even when you don't need it, so that the capability is automatically there when you do.

HOW-TO 4: Dear Diary. Use the illeist diary method to write about your day, a decision you have to make, something that's bothering you, or an opportunity you might have in the near or distant future. This is writing about yourself in second or third person, as though you have become someone else, Coach. No *I*, *me*, or *my*. Use [your name], *he*, *she*, or *they*. Try this exercise a few times a week so it begins to feel natural. If you already journal every day, start incorporating an illeism segment. You'll be able to take Coach's point of view more easily in time, giving you the power to get outside your own head.

When writing, there may be times you're tempted to explain or justify your feelings or point of view. That's fine, just stick with the distanced language. For example, instead of "I felt frustrated," you would write, "Mike felt frustrated because he had spent a lot of time thinking about and preparing for something that didn't pan out." You'll notice this approach has the effect of peeling those feelings, justifications, and defenses away from your objective view of the situation, allowing Coach to provide input. It acknowledges feelings without privileging or judging them. You can now empathize with yourself *and* hold yourself accountable, allowing you to focus on the behavior and decision at hand.

What About *You*?

Participants in many of the studies we've referenced used third or second person in the distanced state, and there doesn't seem to be much of a difference in the effect between the two. *You* is a variation on using third-person pronouns to promote distance, and it's probably one you're more familiar with. It is likely you have urged yourself on at some point during a hard task by using the pronoun *you*. For example, it seems natural to say, "You can do it!" when you feel like there's nothing left in your tank during a long-distance run,[20] or when you're at work late, racing against a deadline. Such phrases work to create the distanced perspective and provide additional motivation.

A study of men accustomed to high-intensity sports tested the effects of distanced self-talk on performance in time trials for a ten-kilometer stationary bicycling exercise.[21] The study also examined each athlete's effort, as measured by the rating of perceived exertion (RPE), an indication of how hard someone is working during activity. Early-training time trials honed participants' self-talk to be motivational and use their own language and ideas as much as possible. In one trial, they used first-person self-talk, and in the other, they implemented second-person distanced language. All participants completed both conditions in random order.

As predicted, using *you* rather than *I* improved the athletes' time. The times using *you* were faster by an average of 23 seconds! (The full time trial took about 17.5 minutes.) What's more, according to the RPE ratings, using *you* did not result in any more perceived exertion than using *I*. Maybe 23 seconds doesn't sound like a lot, but individual races in the Tour de France, the pinnacle of the professional cycling season, are often won by fractions of a second. And the overall race—two thousand miles of cycling, across twenty-one days, over multiple mountains—has been won by less than a minute ten times in its history.

The researchers postulated that when we talk to ourselves using the second-person *you*, it mimics the voice we have heard countless times from parents, teachers, and coaches. "You can do it." "You've got this." This mimicry of encouragement from a trusted authority activates a higher level of obedience and a greater chance of carrying out our intentions. This suggests an additional benefit of deciding as Coach, and then performing as you. Once you (as Coach) decide what you should do, and you (as you) shift back to putting the advice into action, you'll have a greater likelihood of sticking with Coach's plan. You don't want to let Coach down. You're no longer pushing yourself just for you; you're doing it for Coach too.

HOW-TO 5: Address yourself as *you*. This actually helps for an in-the-moment performance boost to get over your stress and see the situation as a challenge to rise to—not a threat to escape. Become Coach and offer yourself encouragement:

▶ "*You* can do it."

▶ "*You're* doing great."

▶ "*You're* pacing yourself well."

▶ "*You've* got a good rhythm."

▶ "*You* are feeling relaxed."

If you have been practicing this linguistic pattern—whether in real time or in a journal, out loud or to yourself, verbally or written—you will be more likely to use it regularly, and it will become second nature.

How to Talk Like Coach

1. **Hey, [your name].** When you're in a stressful situation, address yourself by name the way Coach or a friend would.

2. **Coach makes the call.** When you need to make a decision, become Coach to make the call, and then advise [your name] to do it.

3. **Get psyched.** Before a stressful event, step out of the "*I* thinking" and deliberately write or talk to yourself about it in the third person to calm your nerves.

4. **Dear Diary.** Write in a journal using the third person (*she*, *he*, *they*, or your name) to gain perspective, objectivity, and accountability.

5. **Address yourself as *you*.** When encouraging yourself in performance mode, use the second-person *you* or your name rather than the first-person *I*.

Summary

Our default state is the immersed me-here-and-now perspective. Linguistically, this state is reflected in language where we refer to ourselves in the first person, using *I* and *me*. This immersed state biases us toward a myopic, threatened, defensive, egocentric perspective that creates a host of issues. When we use language Coach would use to talk to us, or that we would use to encourage and support another person, we promote psychological distancing. Distanced talk, even distanced self-talk, invites psychological distance. Distance results in a more open, curious, challenge-seeking mindset that shapes all facets of life, positively impacting learning, decision-making, task performance, relationships, and overall satisfaction.

PART III

Be Somewhere Else

5

Be on the Balcony

*Imagine you're negotiating on a stage and part of your
mind goes to a mental and emotional balcony, a
place of calm, perspective, and self-control.*

—WILLIAM URY, COMMENCEMENT SPEECH AT DAWSON COLLEGE[1]

International cricket has a pecking order. Australia, England, and
South Africa—along with Afghanistan, Bangladesh, India, Ireland, New Zealand, Pakistan, Sri Lanka, the West Indies, and
Zimbabwe—are at the top, all full members of the International
Cricket Council (ICC), founded in 1909. The sport is extremely
popular in these countries, drawing huge crowds, and their teams
win most of the major international tournaments. Then there are
the underdogs, such as the Netherlands, Namibia, Canada, the
United States, and Kenya. Whether because of their population,
culture, or heritage, cricket does not play as strong a role in these
places as it does in the twelve full member nations. These countries,
and ninety-two others, are called "associate nations" because they
have traditionally been associate members of the ICC. Some associate members make the jump to full members, such as when Afghanistan and Ireland did so in 2017. People love rooting for the
underdog, and if the associate nations can level up their game to
take on the big dogs, so much the better for everyone: the fans,

the associate nations, and even the full members. After all, better competitors only improve the game.

One recurrent problem for underdog players in big international tournaments is responding to the pressure they feel at bat against higher rated (and higher paid) players on the big teams. In cricket, coaches typically arrange their batsmen in batting performance order with the best batsman up first. As a consequence, if the earlier batsmen get dismissed, then their weaker teammates are left to get the job done with even less time remaining in the game. It is a double whammy, amplifying the pressure.

Jeremy Snape, a professional English cricket player turned sports psychologist, described the feeling of being at bat to us: "Helmets dripping with sweat, the crowd shouting . . . fielders closing in and restricting your ability to score runs . . . saying anything they can to intimidate you and erode your confidence." Everything is at stake, and it's all on you, right here, right now. The immersed state kicks in. You anticipate what it will look like if you go out, leaving your team with an out and a degraded batting lineup. What will the fan reaction be? What about your professional reputation and salary prospects? The pressure mounts. These thoughts are self-defeating as your focus is hijacked from the task to your image. It's an unhelpful shift, draining resources from what you're there to do: hit the next pitch from the bowler. Even though you spent countless practices preparing, you buckle under pressure.

Each of the full member teams have large staffs, including their own sports psychologist. For the associate nations, the league supplies only a single sports psychologist to serve all the teams. The arrangement could invoke a conflict of interest, as the same coach is helping teams who will compete against each other. Still, it works, because the associate nations share an us-against-them feeling in opposition to the full members.

At the 2007 World Cup held in Barbados, Snape was the sports psychologist for the associate teams. Having been an international cricket player himself, he knew the feeling of acute stress. In one pressure-filled game during his career, he failed at bat in front of a stadium of 120,000 jeering Indian fans. Head down and shoulders slumped, he left the pitch and headed to the balcony, where he immediately heard himself giving sound advice to the next batter: "Relax, breathe, focus on the ball, there's no rush." It was the exact advice he had needed moments earlier. Why hadn't he been able to feel that way when he was out there on the pitch? When he was on the balcony, it was as if he were a different person. He started thinking of this alternate, relaxed, distanced mental perspective as "Balcony Boy."

Motivated to access Balcony Boy at will, Snape pursued a degree in sports psychology, studying the impact of our minds on our performance. The worst feeling, he says, does not come from losing but from not playing the best game we know we are capable of. And he realized that the difference between playing *that* game and the game we actually play is caused entirely by our own mental state, the same state that blocked Intel's Moore and Grove for a year and that caused Captain Lee's disastrous landing.

While Snape pursued his degree, he also played on an English county team in Leicestershire. This gave him the opportunity to test his research and achieve redemption. By developing a series of pre-shot routines, Snape was able to replicate the mental state of Balcony Boy, one that he could enter between pitches. In one finals game, in front of twenty-eight thousand people in the stands, which was airing internationally, it all came down to Snape. As he explained, "My team needed four runs to win in the last few deliveries. . . . I dialed up the 'mental focus' on my pre-shot breathing and counting routine to nine and turned the outcome focus on the scoreboard, the prize money and the media down to one." He kept his focus on task, not on image.

Facing the experienced Pakistani international bowler Azhar Mahmood, Snape could feel the tension creeping in. Mahmood was "deadly accurate," and Snape feared a repeat of his failure in India three years earlier. Snape became Balcony Boy, "so much so that I freed up the part of my brain that played instinctively, and I played one of the best shots in my career to win the game and got carried off by my teammates." Snape was a believer: Balcony Boy worked.

At the 2007 World Cup, Snape saw the same issues among the associate players. After making a self-inflicted error under pressure, they would throw down their bat in the dressing room and yell obscenities. Then they would wipe their face and head out to the balcony to cheer on their teammates for the climax of the game. Something happened when they got out on the balcony. They would feel entirely differently about the player at bat, even though the situation would be more pressing for the team as the runs-to-balls ratio was even worse.

Snape introduced Balcony Boy to the associate teams. They loved it. They got BALCONY BOY T-shirts, they talked about Balcony Boy, and they visualized themselves as Balcony Boy *before* going out to bat. They'd do the same between pitches, settling their minds and allowing them relief from the me-here-and-now immersion that made them so vulnerable to emotional hijack. Balcony Boy worked. As a coach, Snape tackled the players' biggest impediment to peak performance: themselves.

You can probably understand why your perspective sitting on the balcony after you have been at bat is different than while at bat, facing the bowler and surrounded by the other team. But can simply imagining yourself on the balcony looking down at a scene that includes you really have the same effect? In a big way, yes!

Becoming Balcony Boy is to be someone else, but Balcony Boy is *somewhere* else as well. This mental image is one of being on the balcony, looking out at yourself the way Coach looks out at you. Coach stands at the side of the field. Coach has the same visual perspective as Balcony Boy. Coach is physically removed from the field of play. This mental relocation is called spatial distancing. By going to the balcony, you go somewhere else. But you also become someone else, and look at yourself as Coach would.

Negotiating from the Balcony

Not only will strategically timed spatial distance improve performance, the external viewpoint—seeing yourself as part of the whole—and the resulting sense of calm will improve decision-making. Like being a batter in an international cricket tournament, negotiations are a natural trigger for self-immersion. William Ury is a Distinguished Fellow of the Harvard Negotiation Project and coauthor of the bestselling book *Getting to Yes*. In *Getting to Yes*, the authors describe the problems of digging in to a self-immersed position during a negotiation. Once we take a position, we argue for it and defend it. We then identify with it and assimilate that position into the image we have of ourselves. That position could be $100 million for a strategic acquisition (and not a penny more!) or the number of inspections a country is allowed to verify the absence of nuclear weapons. Compromising on our position means giving up a piece of ourselves. It's a loss. In addition to, or even supplanting, the original objective of the negotiation, we now have a new objective: saving face. This is the same shift of focus from task to image that we've seen before.

But Ury has a trick to keep himself focused on the task at hand. It's the same one used by Snape: Go to the balcony. Ury has been involved in some high-level, difficult international negotiations, including nuclear risk-reduction protocols between the United States and Russia. He describes how creating distance between himself and the negotiation works: In the heat of the moment, he likes to take a pause mentally and imagine he's on a balcony, looking down at the negotiations, rather than sitting in his chair at the negotiation table.[2]

You see, negotiators have the same human biases as the rest of us: anchoring, confirmation bias, escalation of commitment, etc. These are easily exaggerated when the situation gets tense and especially if it becomes personal. Naturally, these problems often result in worse outcomes for both sides.[3]

So, Ury pauses and goes to the balcony to create mental space. The pause could be just for the length of a breath or during a natural pause in the conversation. Here's how Ury describes it: "Part of your mind goes to a mental and emotional balcony, a place of calm, perspective, and self-control where you can stay focused on your interests, keep your eyes on the prize." Going to the balcony helps him escape the me-here-and-now immersed perspective and take on Coach's distanced perspective.

HOW-TO 1: Become Balcony Boy. You can do this too. Try it before heading into a stressful situation. Maybe the competition is goading you, critical voices in your head are beating up on you, or you are dug in to a particular position in an argument. Go to the balcony. Do this during a pause in the action—before your performance, before you are up to bat. Take a mental walk onto the balcony and observe yourself from there. You should feel more at ease, focused simply on the task, undistracted by your image, with a calm mix of playfulness, determination, and possibility. Mental teleportation of this type is an underused human superpower.

Fly on the Wall

One study by researchers Özlem Ayduk and Ethan Kross set out to explore the physical effects spatial self-distancing has on our own bodies.[4] Subjects were deliberately invited to replay an event that had made them angry, with instructions to try to understand the emotions that they had felt during the event. Half were given instructions prompting self-immersion: "Relive the situation as if it were happening to you all over again. . . . Reexperience the interaction as it progresses in your mind's eye." The other half were given instructions to self-distance: "Take a few steps back. . . . Move away from the situation to a point where you can now watch the conflict from a distance. . . . Watch the conflict unfold as if it were happening all over again to the distant you." This is very much like seeing themselves from the balcony, only here the participants were thinking about a past event.

Notice that in both conditions, the participants acknowledged the reality of the past event. It happened. The difference is that in the self-distancing group, they simply imagined this happening not to their me-here-and-now self but to a distanced version of themselves. They rewatched the event as though it were happening to someone else.

As expected, those who retold their stories from the distanced perspective reported lower levels of reexperiencing their original feelings. In other words, they were able to stop reliving and ruminating over the painful event. Through distancing, they reconstrued the event, reappraised the situation, and gained some understanding or acceptance. The reframe yielded an elevated perspective. Not only were they able to move on from the upsetting occurrence, their blood pressure was literally lower. Their bodies got the memo.

What is actually happening? We are not denying that bad things happened. That is unhelpful and does not work. Neither are we suggesting that perpetrators should not be held accountable. That is a separate issue. However, past events are just that—*in the past*. They happened and cannot be undone. Acknowledgment is appropriate, but letting them continue to negatively affect our lives only furthers the pain. Distance, acknowledge, decide to accept, and move on.

Now, if we are mentally and physiologically calmer, shouldn't we also be less aggressive? This was the dissertation topic of PhD candidate Dominik Mischkowski at The Ohio State University, along with Ethan Kross.[5] This time they described the distanced perspective as viewing yourself as "a fly on the wall." They were joined in the study by psychologist Brad Bushman, a renowned aggression researcher. Bushman's earlier work used a clever technique to ethically induce and measure aggressive behavior in a laboratory setting. Study participants selected the volume and duration of a blast of noise to play through another participant's headphones.

Participants were separated into three groups: control, distanced, and self-immersed. At the start of the study, everyone was told that their job was to solve fourteen difficult anagrams—taking all the letters of one word to create another—while listening to intense classical music. They were to use an intercom to tell the experimenter once they had solved each problem, and they were given only seven seconds to complete each one. After the fourth problem, the experimenter interrupted them: "Look, I can barely hear you. I need you to speak louder, please." Then, after the eighth problem, they intervened again: "Hey, I still need you to speak louder, please!" And after the twelfth problem: "Look, this is the third time I have to say this! Can't you follow directions? Speak louder!" Those in the immersed group felt angrier, and their actual *behavior* was more aggressive. When they had a chance to blast an opponent with noise, they chose louder settings. Research on this simple mental technique for spatial self-distancing consistently shows that people experience less negative emotion, including anger and depression, and are less likely to rehash painful events. They have lower blood pressure. They even behave less aggressively. The additional effort to perform this mental technique takes about fifteen seconds, but the effects can last a week.[6] It may take just a little more time and effort to achieve a distanced perspective, but the benefits are well worth it.

HOW-TO 2: Be a fly on the wall. When thinking about a past event that is emotionally troubling, consider it from a distanced perspective. Use this tool anytime you relive the same negative experience more than once, without gaining any understanding or the ability to get over it. Step back and move away from the situation, so that you're observing it from the perspective of a fly on the wall. Watch the event happen to the distant you. As a bonus, try to understand the emotions your distant self is experiencing and why that person feels that way. This will help you reconstrue the event in a manner that enables you to gain understanding and move forward.

When you see yourself from the perspective of a fly on the wall or from the balcony, you end up thinking about yourself as a different person. From the spatially distanced perspective, using the third person feels organic. There's a natural tendency toward unprompted illeism. Being somewhere else naturally allows us to be someone else as well.

The Power of Observation

Let's go back to Jen Pierce, the former leader of commodity traders who's now an executive coach. She told us the story of a client of hers, Dr. Carson, a cardiologist. (Some details have been changed to anonymize the story.) A skilled professional, she did not need coaching in her area of expertise. What she did need help with was the constant feeling of being overwhelmed and stressed out. This anxiety was causing her family life to suffer, and she knew she needed a better work–life balance. This, ostensibly, was the reason she sought coaching.

Dr. Carson's practice came with the expected hassles: insurance, billing, turnover, and staffing issues. But according to her, none of those were her fault, just the nature of the industry. These superficial factors, seemingly outside her control, were easy to stress and complain about, but Pierce recognized they were not the real issue, just symptoms of a deeper problem. Pierce hoped to help Dr. Carson recognize that both the real problem and the solution lay in her mind.

When Dr. Carson complained about staff and other related concerns, Pierce told her she didn't want to hear about it. Pierce needed to start somewhere else, leading the doctor through a series of questions to understand the root of her stress. Pierce began by asking about her daily routine: what time she got up in the morning, what she did first thing, what time she got to work, how many patients she saw a day, and for how long. Then Pierce had her focus on her first appointment of the day.

"Where are you right now?" she asked. "What are you doing? Who are you talking to? Are you multitasking? Are you drinking coffee?" Then she got even more specific. "How do you go in there? Do you knock on the door? Do you open the door? Do you stand up or sit down? Do you write on something? Are you just at your computer writing notes? Are you looking the person in the eye? Are you sitting with them? Are you talking with them?"

Recognizing Dr. Carson had only about ten or fifteen minutes to spend with each patient, Pierce wanted her to consider what could happen in that relatively short window. "It takes weeks to get in to see me," the doctor explained. "And people complain, or they can't even get in to see me anyway. But now when I'm with them, I'm going to review the notes in the stupid computer system. I hate this. I hate that I have to spend the time I have with them looking at a computer, and then someone calls in sick and I hate the world."

Pierce asked her to take that a step further. "How are you feeling inside? What is your heartbeat doing? How much caffeine are you drinking? Are you annoyed? Are you happy? Walk me through your day. When do you feel good? When do you feel relaxed?" Dr. Carson replied that she never felt relaxed, that she was always late for the next appointment. "The nurse is telling me, 'Hey, you gotta go,' and I'm wearing my watch and have my hand on the doorknob like I'm trying to get out, but the patient keeps talking. And I'm getting more and more frustrated and annoyed because I'm falling further behind."

As her coach, Pierce was an outside observer. Importantly, though, all the information came directly from Dr. Carson herself. Pierce made a suggestion Dr. Carson would likely not have considered on her own, at least not as long as she stayed in the self-immersed perspective: "Let's try not holding on to the door. Instead, sit down and face the patient. Even though inside, you're dying to get the hell out. Just try it for one day with one set of patients and then measure, How do you feel? How did the patients feel? How far behind were you at the end of the day?"

Choosing to be present with her patients, if only for a few more moments, allowed Dr. Carson to slow down, inviting her to focus and connect with them on a deeper level than before. Pierce suggested she try something similar with the staff: "Do you look them in the eye in the morning? Do you say, 'Good morning'? Do you use their name? Or are you just running around with your head cut off and barking orders at them because this isn't done and that needs to happen?"

Pierce had an observer's perspective, but she relied on what Dr. Carson was able to self-report. Pierce gave the kind of sage advice we give a friend because we see their situation so much more clearly from a distance. After following Pierce's advice, Dr. Carson reported feeling less stressed herself, and her staff had measurably less turnover. She also received better patient reviews. You can do much of this yourself.

HOW-TO 3: Observe [your name's] behavior. You can ask yourself a lot of the same types of questions Pierce asked Dr. Carson. Consider adding a twist: Present them to yourself in the third person. Here are some questions to get you started. You probably have a few of your own to add. When possible, focus the questions on specific behaviors.

▶ When does [your name] get to work? How does [your name] feel when they get there?

▶ When does [your name] actually start working? What does that mean? What does [you name] do before they begin working?

▶ How does [your name] interact and communicate with other people?

▶ If someone were to observe [your name], what would they see?

▶ What does [your name] spend most of their time doing? Which activities are most important?

▶ How does [your name] feel at the end of the workday? What thoughts preoccupy their mind?

Author James Clear talks about the power of observation in his bestseller *Atomic Habits.*[7] Observation is a key starting point for identifying bad habits, eventually breaking them, and forging good habits instead. It all starts by observing yourself as though you're watching someone else. As in, "I see *them* walking straight to their office without making eye contact with anyone else." Or, "Notice how *they* pick up their phone and scroll for several minutes as soon as they sit down at their desk." Or, "I see *them* going to the pantry for a snack instead of choosing the fresh produce." Only after the behavior has been dispassionately observed can you decide to change it. You can think about this as though you're watching a tape of yourself through the eyes of an impartial and supportive coach, simply observing what can be improved.

Watching the Game Tapes

David recalls getting on a plane one evening right after an NFL game wrapped up and finding referees from the game piled into the seats around him. Before the cabin door was even shut, they had opened their iPads to watch the game so that they could critique their own calls. It probably didn't hurt that they had ordered drinks, anesthetizing themselves from the pain of viewing themselves and their decisions on the field. During the Super Bowl that season, he recognized the same head referee and team that had been on the plane. No coincidence.

Coaches and players on any professional or college sports team, even some high school teams, routinely watch recordings of their games or meets. Though it's impossible to know the players' intentions, coaches can observe their behavior.

Logbooks, timelines of actions, recordings of meetings, and videos of speeches all help paint an accurate picture of your performance that can help you learn faster, improve, and make better decisions moving forward. These tools will ground you in truth in a way that your memories will not. Remember, with a question as simple as "What percentage of the work did you do?" our minds actively curate what we recall to enhance our self-image as a good team player. In an effortless and immediate way, you will definitely remember when you came in to work on a weekend (you probably even recall what weekend, how long you were there, and what you were missing out on), but you will likely not remember the time a colleague came in on a weekend without prompting . . . assuming you were even there to notice.

When surgeon Atul Gawande saw that his performance in the operating room had plateaued, he hired a former mentor as a coach to observe him in real time. Gawande describes how the coach noticed aspects of a surgery he had missed entirely: a light moved and was not trained directly on the wound on which he was operating, and his elbow rose up near the level of his shoulder, reducing his ability to control the instrument. His coach did what great coaches do, acting as his "external eyes and ears providing a more accurate picture of reality."

In a 2017 TED Talk, Gawande relayed what his coach told him: "Your elbow goes up in the air every once in a while. That means you're not in full control. A surgeon's elbows should be down at their sides resting comfortably. So that means if you feel your elbow going in the air, you should get a different instrument, or just move your feet."[8] Gawande explained the revelation as "a whole other level of awareness." Convinced that coaching helped him, Gawande applied this model to improving childbirth deliveries in India. Without coaching, less than one-third of the established basic practices in delivery were happening, and there was no improvement over time. With coaching, after four months, measured across 160,000 births, the teams he was working with began performing over two-thirds of the basic practices.

Gawande has been a fan of coaching ever since, and he has studied it closely. In a piece for *The New Yorker*, Gawande spoke with renowned violinist Itzhak Perlman, asking him: If so many top athletes had coaches, why didn't musicians, such as concert violinists?[9] Perlman was not sure, but he let Gawande in on a little-known secret. Perlman had long had his own version of a coach— his wife, Toby, whom he had met at Julliard over forty years earlier. He explained to Gawande: "The great challenge in performing is listening to yourself. Your physicality, the sensation that you have as you play the violin, interferes with your accuracy of listening." The perception musicians have of their music during their performance can vary widely from those of the listener. He told Gawande that his wife is "an extra ear" who can provide input. Of course, this specific instance requires an independent observer. But we can effectively observe most of our behavior ourselves if we can only take on a distanced perspective. We gain our own observational input for self-improvement.

HOW-TO 4: Watch your game tapes. Recall your day. You are seeking objective information and evidence. Watch the scenes as Coach and give yourself the necessary feedback, whether good, bad, or ugly. If Coach could observe your paper trail or digital footprints for the day, what story would they tell? Remember, Coach is supportive but objective. Coach is not concerned about why your arm is entering the water in a certain way or why you go straight for the snack cabinet when you get home from work. Coach just sees the behavior clearly and dispassionately. Then coach yourself on what to do instead.

David has recorded himself swimming as practice for watching himself deliver speeches. He tries to apply the curious, eager, seeking, improving mindset from the swimming video to something more significant, such as a keynote or a conversation with a client. He also uses this technique of self-observation when difficult discussions arise, those that might lead to anger or frustration, which are sure paths to clouding our judgment. When taking this approach, he is often less prone to these negative feelings. Learning a new language? Record yourself and play it back.

It's Not About You

There is an important difference between imagining we're observing ourselves from a distanced perspective in a purposeful, developmental way versus looking at ourselves in a self-conscious way, as though we're taking a selfie. The point here is it's not about your image. It's not about *you*. It's about the task, the situation, the decision you are facing.

Josh Waitzkin, the chess prodigy who inspired the movie *Searching for Bobby Fischer*, reinvented himself as a world-champion martial artist and then again as the author of *The Art of Learning*.[10] He knew well the dangers of the self-conscious observer perspective: "Sometimes I seemed to play chess from across the room, while watching myself think." He realized that he had not fully self-distanced and was not observing himself neutrally, as he would one of the other players. He was watching himself, yes, but still from a self-immersed perspective. Conscious of his fame, he was concerned about what others might think of him and what he physically looked like while he played. His focus on image, not task, undermined his ability to concentrate.

If you find yourself thinking about how you look or what others might think of you, you're doing it wrong. That means you're still stuck in your own head. You have to dislodge yourself and really become that person on the balcony. Really become Coach. Not whoever is evaluating you. Not an audience member. Not the media. An impartial observer from a distance.

Remember, by mentally moving to the balcony or becoming a fly on the wall, you are taking Coach's objective, dispassionate perspective—not your own. That person in the center of the action is *someone else*. You are observing and advising *them*. Coach is focused on the task, not the image.

Still stuck in self-immersion? Keep zooming out. After Apollo 14 astronaut Edgar Mitchell returned from the moon, he said, "You develop an instant global consciousness, a people orientation, an intense dissatisfaction with the state of the world, and a compulsion to do something about it. From out there on the moon, international politics looks so petty. You want to grab a politician by the scruff of the neck and drag him a quarter of a million miles out and say, 'Look at that, you son of a bitch.'"[11] Other astronauts and travelers to space have reported similar experiences. It is common enough to have been labeled the "overview effect."

From space, we look small, insignificant. Our problems seem like mere blips. The things we have in common overwhelm our petty differences. You can simulate this by centering yourself on Google Earth and zooming out, and out, and out. You'll be in good company. Newton imagined being in the stars and looking down at earth. Einstein famously imagined what it would be like to ride a ray of light.

Distance to Embrace Feedback

As you move farther away, the concrete details fade, revealing the basic shapes and patterns. It is the focus on the details that obscures this bigger-picture view. Let's say you agree to play a card game, but when the deck is revealed, you don't recognize the characters on the cards. You have to choose between two cards, with one of them being the winner. It seems random, but not quite. Some cards have better odds than others. The good news is that you get feedback every single time you choose a card—"Correct, you win twenty-five points" or "Incorrect"—so you adjust your selections as you learn the patterns. Now, if you're lucky, you're in the experimental condition of this study, which was led by Cambridge researcher Quentin Dercon.[12] This group watched a ninety-second video on the power of cognitive distancing before the cards were first dealt, and they received the following instructions after each round of the game: "Try to distance yourself from your immediate reaction, by taking a step back from how you are feeling." The control group had the same task but without the self-distancing instructions or video.

It's almost bizarre how this simple mental manipulation helped people pick up on the winning pattern more easily. The reason, according to the study, is the distanced group learned more from the *negative* feedback. Hence, they performed better on the task. And this was especially true as it became more difficult. By observing from the balcony, we can better accept the necessary feedback to improve our performance—even if, and according to this study, especially if, it is negative.

The benefits of taking a mental step back depend in part on us actually learning from the feedback we receive or observe about ourselves. Spatial distancing enables us to take advantage of negative feedback by helping us to not feel defensive, allowing us to learn more. When we're allergic to feedback, it's because we're too self-immersed. By contrast, self-distancing allows us to embrace feedback, course correct, and move forward. And feedback need not be the awkward discussion that follows the dreaded "Can I give you some feedback?" Or the annual performance review at work. We are using the term *feedback* here in a broader sense: information derived from the task itself. For example, how does changing hand position at the front end of a swim stroke affect your distance per stroke?

Think about the best coaches, instructors, teachers, bosses, or mentors you've had throughout life. They didn't just cheer you on in your endeavors; they delivered the hard truths that would help you develop and grow. By observing yourself from a spatial distance, you create the mental space to accept and act on honest feedback without your ego getting in the way.

Other people have the same egoic defense mechanisms that we do, but that means we have the same egoic defense mechanisms that they do. This is a huge inhibitor to clear and honest feedback in the workplace. Even when we ask for it, we are unlikely to get the most useful and honest assessments.

One technique, recommended by Daniel Yudkin and Tessa West in their *Wall Street Journal* article "How to Tell If You're the Office Jerk," suggested asking for feedback relative to ideal behavior rather than about your actual behavior.[13] For example, instead of asking, "Did I give you enough time to make the changes to that document I assigned you?" say, "When it comes to making changes to documents like the one I just assigned you, what's the ideal amount of time for you to get the work done?" This is effective because it allows the other person a bit of separation between the feedback and you. Their response is not a judgment of your behavior, which the other person may suspect will make you defensive, reduce the chance of you acting on the feedback, and possibly damage your relationship.

How to Be on the Balcony

1. **Become Balcony Boy.** View the situation from the balcony in preparation for a stressful event and during pauses in the action. This will enable you to focus on the task rather than worrying about how you look.

2. **Be a fly on the wall.** Replay a negative event while observing yourself from a distance. This will result in reconstruing— or reframing—rather than reliving the painful experience, which aids perspective, understanding, acceptance, and your ability to move on.

3. **Observe [your name's] behavior.** When reviewing your own behavior, think of it as observing a third party. Ask them questions.

4. **Watch your game tapes.** Become Coach and watch the video to observe your behavior without consideration of your motives or excuses. Review electronic records and replay the activities objectively. Then provide actionable feedback.

Summary

Going to the balcony or being a fly on the wall automatically prompts us to exit the immersed me-here-and-now perspective and adopt Coach's perspective. By being somewhere else, we become someone else, reducing the dysfunctional effects of ego. From the distanced perspective, when we observe ourselves, it feels like we are looking at someone else. We see ourselves more clearly, with less distortion. We are focused on the task, not on the image. In this distanced state, we are better able to learn from feedback and make better decisions.

There's another benefit to viewing ourselves from a distance: We can see the bigger picture.

6

See the Big Picture

It's funny how some distance makes everything seem small;
And the fears that once controlled me can't get to me at all.

—ELSA, FROZEN

One of our global partners delivering Intent-Based Leadership training and transformation is Warsaw-based consultancy 4Results, founded by Maciej Trybulec and Sławek Błaszczak. Trybulec's corporate clients often come to him because they want a cultural transformation. Sometimes they are trying to see their way through a specific strategic decision. In these cases, Trybulec conducts an exercise in which he has them imagine they are on a dance floor. He explained to us, "I don't know about you, but I still feel a bit self-conscious when I'm dancing. I don't want to, but I do. So, for me, dancing is a bit performative. There is a strong influence pushing me into the immersed perspective." This feeling is exactly what he is trying to make the participants aware of.

First, Trybulec asks them to write down what they are seeing, thinking, and feeling as they are dancing. By default, they automatically take the first-person, self-immersed perspective, using first-person pronouns *I* and *me*. In the immersed state, they might write, "I see people around me, and I think about how I am moving. It feels like I am comparing myself to them."

Next, Trybulec asks them to imagine they are on the balcony, looking down on the dance floor—that they just happen to be on—and repeat the exercise. With this new instruction, they see the dance floor as a whole, describing the entire scene, such as, "More people are dancing at one end of the floor, and there's a group of people dancing in a line closer to the speakers." Only once they've taken that second broader perspective does Trybulec have the participants think of solutions to the business problem they're there to tackle. He reports that these leaders do so with less emotional involvement, and they come up with more creative solutions than the default immersed "on the dance floor" perspective.

This exercise illustrates an additional benefit of spatially distancing ourselves: Being on the balcony not only helps us create psychological distance but it enables us to see the big picture. This is only natural. The further we are from an object, scene, or dilemma, the more we see it in its entirety. When we think about situations as being further away, we construe them less in terms of their lower-level, specific, concrete, and idiosyncratic features and more in terms of their essential, abstract, and more general qualities. Spatial distance invites us up the construal ladder to a higher level.[1]

HOW-TO 1: Zoom out. Imagine seeing yourself on the dance floor, or in whatever situation you're in. Except don't focus on you. Don't look at you on the dance floor; look at the dance floor that you happen to be on. You are just part of the scene. The result should be that you see the whole of the situation more clearly. Some of the specific details might be blurred, but you can see the fundamental shapes and how they fit together. You have a sense that you are gaining perspective and seeing the big picture. To illustrate this effect, the next time you are looking at a broad landscape or urban scene, relax your eyes for a moment and allow the details to blur. You'll get a sense of the general colors and major shapes. Individual details ought to disappear.

Changing our perspective through spatial distancing helps us transition out of the me-here-and-now self and see ourselves as part of a greater whole. Our own unique sense of self and self-importance is minimized. We are just part of the team, just part of the scene, just part of the action. Imagining ourselves as Coach can automatically trigger this because Coach is off the field. When we take Coach's perspective up there on the balcony, we have a whole new view of the world from which we can make better decisions, whether on the pitch, on the dance floor, or at the negotiation table. We see the field, on which we just happen to be one of the players.

Distance Reveals What Matters Most

Buying a car is a major decision. It's a big expense, second only to owning a home for most families. The purchase affects our daily lives and our overall finances for years. Yet, according to lending tree.com, 39 percent of new car buyers have regrets about their purchase. Let's consider why.

What typically happens when we go to buy a car? We arrive at the dealership, planning to purchase a certain model. We've researched the car online, checked *Consumer Reports*, and spoken with family, friends, and anyone else we know who we think has some useful advice. We head into the showroom with confidence and explain what we're looking for—only to discover that specific model is sold out. "But," the salesperson says with a smile, "we have this other car. . . ." Negotiations ensue. An hour or so later, we walk out, having spent money on features we did not need, a model more expensive than we wanted, or a financing package that reduces monthly payments but increases the total cost. When we bought that car from the dealership, we were there, right in front of the negotiator, mired in the here and now, and fixed by our location. We were wrapped up in the action, mentally and physically. Immersed, we were overloaded with information: options on the vehicle, packages, and financing. If we had created space, it's likely we would have gotten more of what we truly wanted out of the negotiation.

Jun Fukukura and her colleagues ran a series of studies delving into this idea, looking at how distancing can improve decision-making.[2] They presented their Cornell undergraduate students with a distancing manipulation, a decision-making task designed to be overwhelming in terms of details and options, and then compared the students' choices.

Participants were divided into groups who were prompted to think about buying a car where they lived, in Ithaca, New York, or across the country, in Portland, Oregon. There was also a control group, which was not prompted about location. Both location-prompted groups were overloaded with the same information about the myriad features of the hypothetical cars. After a brief period, they were asked which car they should buy. The details were too complex to analyze comprehensively in the time allowed: twelve attributes (e.g., gas mileage, sound system, cup holders) varied across four different fictitious vehicle makes (e.g., a Hatsdun or a Nabusi). There was an optimal solution, which was the brand that had the attributes most valued by consumers in general. For example, gas mileage is more important than the number of cup holders to most people.

The information overload took its toll: 63 percent of the participants buying locally did not make the optimal choice. But for the distanced group thinking about buying the car over two thousand miles away in Portland, only 31 percent made the suboptimal choice. What about the control group that was not prompted either way? The result was essentially the same as the home city group, 61 percent did not make the optimal choice. The control group results mimicked the local group. This is unsurprising supporting evidence that the immersed state is our default. Without being told where we should think about buying a car, we automatically think about buying a car where we are. The authors sum up the study: "Thus, when confronting a decision with many pieces of information, people may improve their decision outcome by self-inducing psychological distance."

This improvement is chalked up to a greater reliance on "gist memory." Under the distance manipulation, students were less bogged down by the noisy and intractable details and were able to perceive, retain, and recall the most important features. In short, the experiment showed that distance helps us make better decisions by letting us focus on more abstract general principles. So, zooming out does not just allow for a better view of ourselves—but of the whole picture at hand.

For example, take the size of a cell phone. You are told that it is 4.5 inches high, 2.3 inches wide, and 0.3 inch in depth. In time, you will forget the numbers, but you are likely to remember that it is compact.

Get the Gist

We know that the best negotiators, like William Ury, use spatial separation to "be on the balcony." The motivation for this type of separation is to achieve psychological distance and emotional regulation. But distance, and perceived distance, helps us see the big picture as well. Professor Marlone Henderson at the University of Texas at Austin studies the effects of spatial distance on negotiation outcomes. One of his studies had participants negotiate the sale of a custom motorcycle.[3] The bike could vary on features and items of importance to the buyer and seller, such as financing, taxes, warranty, and delivery date. When features have different levels of importance to the buyer and the seller, it's more possible to achieve win-win solutions, known as "integrated resolutions" in the study of negotiations. In a real estate transaction, for example, perhaps the seller cares more about timing and the buyer cares more about price. With an effective negotiation, the seller gets a quicker closing and the buyer gets a cheaper price. Win-win.

Henderson employed a simple manipulation in his study to measure the effects. The mock negotiations were conducted via text exchanges. He led some participants to believe they were several thousand feet away from their negotiation counterpart, whereas others were told their counterpart was just a few feet away. Since this was a text negotiation and the negotiators never met, why would it matter? Participants could not tell either way. The outcome? Those who believed they were far apart had more integrated resolutions than those who thought they were close by. Crazy. With imagined distance, negotiators focused more on abstract principles, as opposed to specific minutiae, leading to better results.

When you see something from afar, it looks smaller. As the details blur, you can still recognize the shape. Flying into Paris, the Eiffel Tower might be visible in the distance. You can't make out the individual steel girders, much less the individual rivets holding them together, but that spire above the cityscape is unmistakable. This blurring of the concrete, specific details while retaining the overall shape elevates your thinking about the object to a higher level of abstraction. This allows you to appreciate the iconic elegance that defines this thousand-foot structure built in 1889.

This higher construal level is another reason why being on the balcony works. When we zoom out, we remove ourselves from the immediate self-immersion of the negotiation and focus on our interests, rather than being attached to our specific position. While distancing requires us to take a pause and step out of the negotiation, at least mentally, we can practice spatial distancing in advance of the negotiation, look for natural breaks, or create our own pause in the action.

Interestingly, in the case of the *Challenger* launch decision in January 1986, it was the Morton Thiokol engineers, physically removed from NASA, who were arguing against launch. Unfortunately, the reports they sent to try to convince the NASA administrators were mired in details, and the government agency remained unconvinced. NASA went ahead with the launch, and *Challenger* exploded seventy-three seconds into the flight, killing all seven astronauts on board.[4]

This accident has been a staple of business school decision-making case studies. Let's recall the context: Ronald Reagan was president, and the United States and the Soviet Union were in the midst of the Cold War. In 1985, Mikhail Gorbachev had become general secretary of the Communist Party. The year 1986 was supposed to be a big one for NASA, with twelve total launches—one shuttle launch per month—and here we were getting to the end of January with the launch already delayed due to cold weather and its effect on the O-ring seals.

The Morton Thiokol engineers—who were remote from the

launchpad and the decision—had a sense that the odds were against launch. Their distanced perspective enabled them to see that, but they needed to convince the decision-makers at NASA, who were reluctant to cancel the launch without detailed evidence that it was unsafe. That would be near impossible because the evidence was not seen clearly in the details but rather in the overall gist of the situation.

Just like it would have been hard for the people participating in Fukukura's car-buying study to explain why they made the decisions they made, the engineers struggled to make their case. Just saying "we have a bad feeling about this" was not convincing. One important note here is that these were not uninformed remote observers. They were intimately involved in the design and manufacture of the solid rocket boosters and the O-rings.

As we all know, the launch and failure happened. The US government's Rogers Commission investigation into the accident succinctly reported: "The joint seal problem was recognized by engineers in both NASA and Morton Thiokol in sufficient time to have been corrected by redesigning and manufacturing new joints before the accident on January 28, 1986."[5]

It is tempting to think that the details we know are more important than the bigger-picture comparisons someone with a distanced view has to offer. But this is a cognitive trap. Dismissing information or advice simply because it comes from a distance is unwise.

HOW-TO 2: Decide from a distance. When you have a complex decision with lots of moving parts, take a moment to imagine yourself making this decision from a remote location. What does this place look like? Mentally travel there and allow for a snap insight to come to mind. It might be an uncomfortable one. Do not dismiss it. This is your gist processing at work.

This tool can be especially useful when you are engaging in an in-person negotiation. It doesn't have to be someone trying to sell you a car or a house; it could be someone at work pressuring you to make a call without enough information or a friend trying to convince you about upcoming plans. Call time-out and create spatial distance either mentally or physically to avoid this cognitive trap.

The reason being somewhere else works is because, fundamentally, it creates psychological distance. We *feel* further removed from whatever it is we're focused on. This psychological distance helps us construe the situation at a higher level of abstractness. We engage in more top-down processing, and we're able to see the big picture. When we mentally relocate ourselves, we see the gestalt. We get the gist. This is the reframe that gives us a better perspective to make big decisions.

Rotate the World or Relocate You?

Imagine a simple dining room. In the middle sits a sparsely set square table with two candles atop. From where you stand, you see the candles next to each other, side by side, one on the left and one on the right. Now imagine the candles in line with each other, one behind the other.

Note that you likely haven't changed *your viewpoint* of the room; you have merely mentally moved the candles so they are now in line. Perhaps you repositioned them, or maybe you rotated the candles or the table they sit on. In any of these cases, maintaining your position while moving the candles or the table is known as "object rotation." We view ourselves as fixed and the objects as moving. It is an egocentric, or autocentric, frame of reference.

Now try the exercise another way. Imagine that the candles and table remain stationary but that *you* move to a different part of the room, so you can see the candles from a new angle, one behind the other. This approach is more cognitively demanding. It takes slightly longer to think about it this way. Seeing the candles as fixed and ourselves as moving is an example of "viewer rotation." It is an allocentric (the root *allo-* means "other") frame of reference, in which we are focused on others rather than on ourselves.

In the first instance, you maintain yourself as the default frame of reference and manipulate the world around you. In the second, you maintain the world as is and manipulate your position in it. This second way may take more effort, but mentally moving yourself is a more effective reframe.

When our neurons are called upon to work, they require increased oxygen, resulting in greater blood flow to activated regions of our brains. This additional oxygen can be measured externally via fMRI. When Simon Lambrey and his colleagues at University College London took fMRI measurements of people performing these two different types of visual manipulations—rotating the objects (egocentric) or repositioning themselves (allocentric)—different parts of the brain lit up, confirming that these are two distinct processes and that repositioning yourself is more powerful.[6]

When we reposition ourselves, our view of the environment changes. In the dining room example, how the furniture behind the table or windows in the wall look will change in relation to how we move ourselves around the room but will not change if we just reposition the candles on the table. Imagining ourselves on the balcony triggers Coach's viewpoint, so we see ourselves in the context of our environment, relationships, and others. The reason we want you to become Coach and then advise yourself is because of the more powerful mental process involved. If we were to simply ask an imaginary Coach what *we* should do, the process is largely egocentric. You yourself have not changed your view, so any answer you get will still be from your own perspective. It's therefore important to relocate yourself—get up on the balcony—to inhabit Coach's perspective and see the bigger picture, unencumbered by the self. This reframe ensures we leave self-immersion behind, so that we get a clearer read on whatever it is we are facing.

HOW-TO 3: Move yourself, not the object. To maximize psychological distance, mentally reposition yourself—not the object, issue, or situation. Let's say you are engaged in a negotiation or have to make a decision about a particular course of action, for example, launching a project or continuing to test and develop it. Mentally relocate yourself to the balcony. Or maybe you are leading a team review or postmortem of a recent event. Conduct it as if you were far away. "Hey, let's imagine we are a new team in Jakarta. What would we want to know from this recent experience?" This invokes a be someone else as well as a be somewhere else reframe.

Remember, the point of this spatial relocation exercise is that you benefit more from changing your mental location than remaining stationary and thinking of things as being farther away from you. This will take more mental effort, but it will be more effective.

Not Just Farther but Higher

Notice that many of these vantage points invoke a higher as well as farther repositioning. This probably comes so naturally that you don't realize you are moving higher as well as farther away. While most coaches might actually be on the sidelines, on the same level as the field, imagine yourself as Coach looking down at yourself on the field of play, as if Coach is up in the commentators' box. You can go higher still. Think of the Apollo photograph of the earth from the moon. View yourself from the Hubble telescope. You're Coach, but maybe you're an astronaut or a Martian, looking down on you and seeing yourself as part of something much bigger.

This is the concept of mental levitation. Imagine you're driving to work and someone in front of you is going painfully slow. You cannot get around them. You start feeling increasingly frustrated. Maybe you even wish you could just run them off the road and go on your merry way. Now zoom out and up: You see the car you're driving, an angry and impatient driver behind the wheel, obsessing about getting to the office thirty seconds sooner. The car in front is carrying a family, talking excitedly because the kids are going to a new school for the first time today. You can see the frustrated driver (you) behind them, red in the face and bug-eyed, looking pretty foolish. Now levitate even higher. These are just two cars in a long string of traffic that goes way past your office. You're just part of the traffic. A German transportation campaign took this message to the streets, with roadside signage saying YOU'RE NOT STUCK IN TRAFFIC—YOU ARE THE TRAFFIC.[7]

Mental levitation allows us to see the bigger picture, see more abstractly. In a study on job choice, participants were asked to imagine they were at a job fair on the top floor of a tall building or to imagine that they were at the same job fair on a lower floor. They were then asked to choose between two managerial positions, one that focused on implementation details and another that focused on bigger-picture business planning. Those who imagined making the decision from the higher location were more likely to select the bigger-picture business planning position. The imagined elevation resulted in thinking at a higher level of construal.[8]

When we are farther away from something, it looks smaller. As Patrick House writes in *Nineteen Ways of Looking at Consciousness*, we know the distant object is not actually smaller. A cat down the hall is the same size as the cat next to me, but my brain presents it as smaller in part because, being farther away, it has less relevance to me, less chance of harming me. Similarly, when we imagine ourselves farther and higher away, our visual image of our immediate surroundings—those practical matters that are weighing on our decisions—seem smaller too. The details are less important, immediate threats become remote, and we are left with what really matters to us.

HOW-TO 4: Levitate! When you need to make a decision, reframe by imagining your vantage point is not just farther out but higher up as well: a hot-air balloon, the top of a mountain, outer space. Look down from afar and see yourself in the context of the whole situation. Are you the traffic? What do you see that you didn't see before?

How to See the Big Picture

1. **Zoom out.** When you zoom out, focus on the situation as a whole, not on you or your image. You are merely part of the scene.

2. **Decide from a distance.** When you're facing a complex problem, mentally travel to a place far from where you are and consider what you might do from there.

3. **Move yourself, not the object.** Achieve spatial distance by mentally moving yourself away from the situation, rather than moving the situation away from you. It is cognitively harder but more impactful.

4. **Levitate!** When relocating yourself, imagine that you are moving to a farther *and* higher vantage point.

Summary

Spatial distancing is a powerful way to change how we see a problem and unlock thinking at a higher level of construal. Because our visual system is connected with our cognition and emotion, we can use mental imagery to move ourselves away from a situation to see it from a distanced, neutral perspective. Being somewhere else promotes bigger-picture thinking. We reframe by zooming out to see the whole context with greater clarity and balance, enabling us to make better decisions.

PART IV

Be Sometime Else

7

Be Your Future Self

I knew when I was eighty I was not
going to regret having tried this.

—JEFF BEZOS, ON FOUNDING AMAZON

In 1994, Jeff Bezos had a lucrative job at a Wall Street firm, a brilliant supportive boss, and was on track to have a successful career. Then he read about this new thing called the internet. At the time, it was growing 2,300 percent a year. He realized that the internet would be big, and he wanted to start a company selling something online that would ride the growth of this new technology. But that would be risky, and he already had a pretty good life. What should he do?

"I came up with this idea," Bezos recounted.[1] "The idea initially was very simple: It was to sell books online, and I went to my boss, who I liked a lot (his name was David), and I said I have this idea to start this company to sell books on the internet." David was open to hearing about Bezos's plan and invited him to explain the details during a long stroll in Central Park. David thought it was a good idea, but as Bezos recalled, with a major caveat: "It would be a better idea for somebody who didn't already have a good job." Maybe David was trying to keep a good employee, or maybe he was just humoring Bezos, but his words got Bezos thinking.

"That made a certain amount of sense to me," said Bezos, "and he [David] said, Why don't you think about it for two days before you make a final decision? And so I went away and I thought about this, and I was trying to figure out how to make this decision because in the moment personal life decisions, those decisions, can be very challenging. And I finally figured out for me the right way to think about it, which was I wanted not to have regrets."

Bezos pictured himself at eighty years old, looking back on his life, reflecting on his decisions and his path. From that future vantage point, he imagined thinking back about whether he would regret leaving the company and missing out on his annual bonus and other considerations, the here-and-now possibilities. "And I thought, You know what, when I'm eighty, I'm not going to think about that. I'm not even going to remember it, but what I do know for a fact [is] if I don't try, I'm going to regret having never tried. And I know also if I try and fail, I'll never regret having tried and failed, and as soon as I thought about it that way, I knew I had to give it a try."

As Bezos described it, he wanted to mentally get out of his me-here-and-now self and imagine himself at eighty. Now inhabiting his future self, he looked back on the decision and saw clearly the path he wanted to take. It worked out. He's one of the richest people in the world, the founder and executive chairman of a company that does $1.58 billion in sales per day, or $18.3 million in sales per second.[2]

Why did this work? Because we think of our future self as a different person. So, when we imagine ourselves as our future selves, we automatically become someone else. Also, this future self is a different *me* with a highly valuable viewpoint, a perspective that is closer to the ideal self. In other words, our future self is a better version of us.

For Bezos, that perspective enabled him to fully grasp what was truly important—living without regret—while the details that seemed so crucial in the present—a well-paying job, a good boss, and a year-end bonus—faded away.

This more ideal version of ourselves that we access by becoming our future self works through three channels. First, we fast-forward closer to the end of our life. The view from the rocking chair affords us a perspective we may not otherwise have: our end-of-life self focuses on what is most important to us in the grand scheme of things. In addition to the radical shift toward what truly matters, this casts us on to the far side of whatever decision we are facing.

This has the effect of flipping our focus from our natural risk aversion and our fear of losing to our fear of regret and chances not taken. When we look forward to decisions that are fundamentally about continuing our current path or doing something new—keeping the same job or finding a new one; living in one place or moving to another—the brain knows that the safe thing to do is to stay the course. After all, doing what we have always done hasn't killed us yet. So, an anti-action bias develops, nudging us to stick with the status quo. However, when we are on the far side of the decision looking back, the opposite happens. We now think of the active option as a missed opportunity.

Second, when we self-distance by becoming our future self, our ideals—what we really desire and value in life—rise in salience relative to the day-to-day practicality and logistics of our current reality. This changes what goes on the scale, and the relative importance of each factor, when we weigh one option versus another.

By changing our time-based point of reference, we inoculate ourselves from the present moment-biased effect of temporal discounting that we are otherwise subject to. The temporal distance reduces the importance and even the visibility of practical constraints. We do not feel them. When those practical constraints fade away, what we are left with is our ideal self. It is almost always a better human and allows us to focus on what we care most about, distinct from the urgent hassles, compromises, concessions, and justifications of today.

In contrast, when we are self-immersed, our day-to-day decisions are constrained by our practical circumstances. We might believe that giving blood is a worthwhile activity, and we may see ourselves as "the kind of person who gives blood." The problem is that we are influenced by the practicalities of finding time to do it. We end up compromising on how we believe we should act in an ideal situation.

Third, becoming our future self enhances our self-control. Or maybe a better way to think about it is that it obviates the need for effortful self-control. Self-control failure is when we make a choice that is different from what we said we wanted beforehand or afterward; for example, losing our temper or making a poor and impulsive health choice. It is a symptom of lack of empathy for our future selves because we see that version of us as a different person, and all that matters is now. Becoming our future self helps to align our decisions and behaviors with what is important to us, creating a more intentional and cohesive whole.

Night Guy Screws Morning Guy

A classic stand-up piece by Jerry Seinfeld, immortalized through the opening credits of his smash sitcom *Seinfeld*, describes how our me-here-and-now self sees our future self as a different person.

> I never get enough sleep. I stay up late at night because
> I'm Night Guy. Night Guy wants to stay up late! What
> about getting up after five hours of sleep? Oh, that's
> Morning Guy's problem. That's not *my* problem. I'm
> Night Guy. I stay up as late as I want.
> See, Night Guy always screws Morning Guy.

The brilliance of Seinfeld's bit and the reason we can all relate to it so well is that it captures our natural tendency to see our future self as someone else. It's not us. "They" can deal with that later.

Emily Pronin—the psychologist introduced earlier who studies the asymmetry between how we see ourselves and how we see others—found that people were four times as likely to describe a meal their future self would eat decades in the future in the third person, using *he* or *she* rather than *I*.[3] Sure, at some level we know that's "us" eating that meal, but that's not really how we talk or act—or how our neurons fire.

Research by UCLA Anderson School of Management professor and behavioral scientist Hal Hershfield found that brain patterns back up this use of third-person language. As he explains in his book *Your Future Self*,[4] MRI scans of people thinking about their future self mimic the brain patterns of people thinking about strangers, rather than themselves.

No Regrets

Bronnie Ware was a hospice nurse in Australia. Although it wasn't a job she specifically sought, she found herself taking care of terminally ill patients. These people were typically in the last three to

twelve weeks of life and had chosen to die at home. It was emotionally taxing work, but Ware found she was good at it, mostly
because of her ability to listen to her patients. As she did, she noticed a set of patterns about their regrets as they approached the
end of their lives. In her thought-inducing book *The Top Five Regrets of the Dying*, she reports what she found.[5]

The number-one regret was, "I wish I'd had the courage to
live a life true to myself, not the life others expected of me." It is a
regret of omission, of the roads not taken. Ware explains: "When
people realise that their life is almost over and look back clearly on
it, it is easy to see how many dreams have gone unfulfilled. Most
people had not honoured even a half of their dreams and had to
die knowing that it was due to choices they had made, or not
made. Health brings a freedom very few realise, until they no longer have it." Ware hopes that we will learn from these stories of
regret to act more courageously to live fuller lives. That is certainly
laudable, but here's the problem: An exhortation to act more courageously is unlikely to work because it does not change how we
think about something. It is akin to yelling "Do better!" at yourself and expecting results.

To act courageously, to shift the bias from inertia or risk avoidance to action, fast-forward your life until you are on the other
side of the decision and look back. When you look back at a decision you made, your mind will frame it in a way that highlights
the regrets, causing you to ask yourself, Why didn't I . . . ? or say,
I wish I had done . . . This regret framing makes the cost of inaction more salient.

Fast-forwarding into the future also puts us closer to our own
death. Much as we might not want to accept it, we will get older,
less mobile, and less energetic. This proximity to the end puts
things in perspective, and the will to act comes more easily. Con-

sider the case of Adam Williams, who played football at Rice University from 1996 to 2000. He retired from his football career after college but stayed in shape, going on to win four medals in natural bodybuilding. After sitting out for eighteen years, at the age of forty he returned to playing American football in Europe for the Amsterdam Crusaders. He lived out this dream for two years. Williams is an inspiration to many and now serves as a personal trainer. He poses this question to his clients and social media followers: "When you are eighty and in a rocking chair, do you want to be able to say you gave it everything you had?"

In Charles Dickens's 1843 novella *A Christmas Carol*,[6] the Ghost of Christmas Future drags miserly Ebenezer Scrooge through time even beyond his death. In this far-distant future, Scrooge sees a sad tombstone unkept and presumably forgotten. As the Ghost takes Scrooge around London, he hears people who are happy he is gone and joking over his misfortune. It is a striking vision of his fate. Worse yet, he finds that Tiny Tim, the son of his employee Bob Cratchit, has died because his family was unable to afford the medical bills to treat his illness. This vision of his future self is incongruent with the person he wants to be. The dream has the intended effect. When Scrooge awakens—was it just his imagination or were those specters real?—he changes his ways, going immediately to help the Cratchit family. By time traveling to his future, he realizes he has to change his present to avoid his regrets later in life.

HOW-TO 1: Fast-forward to the far side. When you think about strategic life decisions—such as starting companies, changing jobs, moving, or retiring—where you are faced with a choice between the status quo and action, imagine you are looking back on it from far into the future and the decision has already been made.

What do you wish you had done? What would you regret not doing? That's your answer.

Elle Cordova is a musician, writer, and self-professed nerd who offers witty commentaries on the intersection of technology, life, and culture. One of her most watched videos is a comedic discussion among "fonts hanging out," ranging from the classic default (and still our personal favorite) Times New Roman, the futuristic Futura, and the relaxed Comic Sans. She plays all of them.

A photo Cordova posted on Instagram in November of 2023 shows us what it's like to time travel. She walks us into the future, to see our current selves more clearly and with greater appreciation. She takes us on this journey gradually, by imagining the dawn of the next day, and then this repeats and speeds up. Years pass. Holidays, events, deaths of friends and families. We become older and older, until we arrive at our last stop—our last day on earth. Lying in a bed, hooked up to machines, we're unsure whether we will see the next day. But we can access our memories clearly and pick a day of our choosing to relive. We pick today, and what a luxury it is to be able to relive today, in our current body, yet with the consciousness of our future self. This is what it's like to become our future self to gain perspective on our current situation.

Short-Term Practicality

People generally don't save enough money today because they overvalue financial decisions close in time and undervalue those far away in time. For example, a 2021 study by Saurabh Bhargava and Lynn Conell-Price tested ways to increase people's enrollment savings in company 401(k) plans.[7] An immediately available ten-dollar gift card was a more effective incentive to enroll than the delayed, though much larger, matching contributions offered by the company that would not be available for years.

David saw this temporal discounting effect hit home in the navy following the end of the Cold War. The navy had more personnel than needed and went through a period of downsizing. People who were near twenty years of service and on the verge of earning lifetime retirement benefits—health care for life and a pension, government paid and indexed to inflation—were offered lump sums to exit at that point, giving up those benefits in return. Many did, forgoing the more lucrative (even calculating for the time value of money) retirement and saving taxpayer money. The military retirement plan has since changed, and a partial lump sum payout to forgo a percentage of retirement pay is now a standard option. We suspect that many veterans take this money, intending to invest it and make more than they would from the retirement program, but they likely do not fully value the inflation protection and backing by the US government. They end up worse off. Companies that are downsizing make their employees similar offers, tempting people to take a lump sum now instead of the longer-term payoff.

If you are a US citizen, then you have or will face the same type of decision when it comes to electing when to draw Social Security benefits. In the US system, withdrawals are elective starting as early as age sixty-two and are mandatory once you reach age seventy. Delaying receiving benefits is rewarded by a benefit payment that is about 75 percent higher at age seventy than at the first opportunity around age sixty-two. For most people, the increase in benefit is disproportionally large, even when accounting for the reduction in the number of payments.

A *New York Times* article reported that while 90 percent of people would benefit from waiting to collect benefits at age seventy, only 10 percent do.[8] The average money lost over one's lifetime is $182,370. Who claims early? People with high degrees of loss aversion.

The good news is interventions similar to becoming one's future self help nudge people toward delaying their withdrawal by focusing on both the potential benefits of waiting and the fear of regret for claiming early. It is harder to sabotage our future self when we temporally distance by becoming that person before making a decision.

Seeing our future self as a different person also renders us more willing to make commitments for the future that we would not agree to do today or tomorrow. Hey, could you serve on the committee on committees starting this week? Sorry, my plate is full. How about next semester? OK.

Like Night Guy, we are happy to outsource inconvenience and hardship to our future self. When asked how much distasteful fluid they would drink for a scientific experiment now versus in the future, people assigned themselves more bitterness later. The more self-immersed we are, the less we identify with our future self, the less we save, the lower our academic scores, and the poorer our health choices—on the whole, we make worse decisions. We need to distance from the me-here-and-now self in order to be true to our ideal self. But the point isn't about forcing yourself to do a task you don't want to do; the reframe allows you to see clearly the work you actually do want to do, and to prioritize that over less important but urgent-feeling chores or distractions. The me-here-and-now self is a pragmatic self, whereas our future self is an ideal self. The pragmatic self is concerned with immediate practical issues and feasibility. (If I only stay up till 1 a.m., I can still get five hours of sleep and make it through the day tomorrow.) The ideal self is more motivated by values, rewards, and desirability.

When we contemplate an action in the future, the concrete practicalities of the behavior are less visible and their perceived contribution to the action are reduced. This leaves behind the dispositional motivations as the explanation. Therefore, we are more likely to discount practical constraints on future behavior and think that we (and others) would act based on values, which represent a more moral and ideal person. This is why we have stronger feelings of moral outrage (and willingness to help others) about future behavior than present behavior.[9] Our future self has no excuse not to "do the right thing."

Wish I Did This Sooner

Procrastination—whether staying up too late or putting off an important project—is a classic example of the me-here-and-now self sabotaging the future self. It is, at heart, a self-control failure. Research by behavioral economist Dan Ariely, author of *Predictably Irrational*,[10] found that externally set deadlines motivate better student progress and results as compared to self-set deadlines—unless those self-set deadlines mirror the even spacing of the externally set deadlines. So, when we gain the perspective of our future self's dispassionate view of the calendar, it mirrors that of an external deadline and helps us overcome self-control failures. Procrastination is exposed for what it is: a lack of empathy for ourselves. It is a thief you have invited to steal time, energy, and success from your future self. Instead, we need to identify and empathize with our future self.

A study by Yuta Chishima and Anne Wilson (2021) of Wilfrid Laurier University in Canada, published in the journal *Self and Identity*,[11] found that when high school students wrote to their future selves, and then reversed the perspective and had their future self write back to them, they felt closer to their future selves. This closeness with the future self manifests in better long-term decision-making.

HOW-TO 2: Become pen pals with your future self. In your letter to your future self, describe the problem you're facing or the decision you need to make. Include the details you must consider, how the decision will affect you and your organization, and your current thoughts. Then answer it *as* your future self.

To test the idea that connection with our future self helps us make better long-term decisions, Hal Hershfield presented people with pairs of circles. The first represented one's current self, and the second represented one's ten-years-in-the-future self.[12] There were seven such pairs, and the pairs ranged from "not overlapping at all" to "overlapping completely." He asked people to select the pair that showed the degree of overlap between their current and ten-year future self. Those who picked the circles with more overlap had accumulated 35 percent more financial assets than those who picked the less overlapping circles. In his book, *Your Future Self*, Hershfield provides further evidence of benefits when participants visualized themselves in the future, such as more ethical decision-making, greater life satisfaction, and better health choices.

The great thing is, we can easily manipulate our future-self continuity, or our connection with our future self. In his virtual reality (VR) lab, Hershfield had students face a mirror in which a digital avatar of themselves looked back at them and reflected their every move and expression.[13] If they lifted their hand to wave, smiled, or frowned, so would the VR avatar. Half the participants saw a non–age-adjusted avatar, whereas the other half saw a seventy-year-old version of themselves. After interacting with the mirror for at least a minute, the students were asked a series of questions by a research assistant, such as "Where are you from?" to help them better identify with their avatars.

Afterward, the students removed their VR headsets and completed a task in which they allocated an imagined thousand-dollar-windfall into four categories: buy something nice for someone else, invest in retirement, plan a "fun and extravagant occasion," or deposit the money into a checking account. Those who had seen their future-self avatar put more than twice the amount into retirement as those who had seen their current-self avatar.

HOW-TO 3: Project yourself into the future. It could be six months; it could be sixty years. What are you doing? How are you dressed? What concerns you now? What's important to you? If you're having trouble envisioning that self, take a cue from Hershfield and use aging software to get an idea of what you will look like in time. You don't need VR goggles either; there are free apps for your smartphone, for example, that provide a filter for your photos to see what you might look like in the future.

Even though we naturally lack empathy for our future self, we can solve this problem instantly through mentally becoming our future self. This is the vantage we want so that we can make wiser life decisions. Then we can take action *now*, which will benefit our future selves *later*. We do not fall into the trap of procrastinating now, for example, and committing ourselves to a later action. The distinction is crucial.

Make sure any decisions you make now from your future self's perspective are an easy default when it's time to follow through. Otherwise, you're just setting yourself up for disappointment in your own unfulfilled promises later. So, if you want to cancel your free trial of a streaming service twelve months from now, put it on the calendar, along with all the information you need to cancel. It's a note to your future self, aiding them in a way to make that action nearly automatic. Even if we're talking about changing a habit that we know we cannot break overnight, we can at least start observing and calling out that habit today.

HOW-TO 4: Act now, not in the future. As much as possible, do the action now. For example, you can prepack your lunch, work bag, or gym bag for tomorrow. Predraft the letter you just decided your future self would write. Put your new commitment on the calendar, not on a to-do list. Set up the auto draft for the savings account, even if you start with only one dollar. Do this when expedient, such as when you already have the bulk of the information in front of you or when you're particularly excited about something.

Having developed a bias for action in a predetermined direction for your future self, you may need to confirm or revise the decisions you initially made once you arrive at that future version of you. That said, it is much easier to tweak the execution from there than it is to start from scratch. Inertia. Your future self will thank you.

Becoming Your Future Self

Our ability to imagine being separate from our current position in time and space is a critical part of our concept of self.[14] Once we think of ourselves as an abstraction, we can manipulate that image in different ways. When you imagine yourself as Coach, you are manipulating the image you have of yourself, just as when you imagine yourself as an older version of you.

When you imagine you are your future self, looking back to

now and asking, What do I wish I would have done on that day? you not only invite yourself to think about a longer-term perspective on the decision but the vantage point also distances you from your current self. If you try it, you can actually *feel* the difference in your thinking between projecting from now to the future or from the future to now. The latter takes more mental effort, but this added effort helps us exit our me-here-and-now self and gain a new perspective.

To test which is more effective, Hershfield and colleagues ran another study, this time using a college savings app called UNest.[15] They contacted twenty-five thousand people who had begun signing up for the app but never finished the sign-up process. To one group, they sent a fast-forward message: "The year is 2021. Move forward to 2031." To the other group, they sent a rewind message: "The year is 2031. Rewind back to 2021." The rewind group was twice as likely as the fast-forward group to complete the process of enrolling in the savings account.

Remember the rotating-candles-on-the-table exercise? It was less natural and more effortful to relocate ourselves and our mind's eye around the table to align the candles (viewer rotation) than it was to simply mentally rotate the candles or the table itself (object rotation). However, viewer rotation was a more impactful change of perspective. There is a parallel here with mentally moving to the year 2031 and then rewinding back (viewer rotation) versus staying in the year 2021 and fast-forwarding to 2031 (object rotation). It takes more mental effort to get out of one's own time and space, but this added effort carries the benefit of greater psychological distance and an improved vantage point. Becoming your future self and rewinding from there is more powerful.

Harvard psychologist Daniel Gilbert studied people's ability to estimate change in themselves looking forward versus looking backward. People readily see large differences between their current self and their past self (looking backward), but they predict only minimal changes for their future self (looking forward).[16] It's much more adaptive to think of ourselves as capable of change. This exercise of thinking backward gives us a better idea of how much we can grow moving forward.

HOW-TO 5: Think backward. Recall what you were like ten years ago. How much have you changed? What has happened that you were not able to foresee then? What advice would you have for yourself? Do you see how much you've grown in the past ten years? Now assume that type of growth potential in your future self when you're considering a decision today.

Such an exercise should put things in perspective, but sometimes ten years may be too close or too far out in time. Different types of decisions will require different time horizons. Choosing where to have lunch this afternoon versus whether or not to take that new job has varying levels of importance and scope, so the amount of temporal distance required to put each in perspective will vary.

Mario Andretti was born in 1940 in Croatia, then part of Italy. After the war, his family relocated to an internally displaced persons camp in Tuscany. When he was fifteen, his parents decided to move to America. At this point, Andretti had his heart set on being a race car driver, but he did not speak any English and he did not know if they even had car racing in America. Those nine days crossing the Atlantic were a very tough time for the teenager.

Sixty years later, after winning races in different kinds of cars, on different kinds of tracks over a span of four decades, he wrote a letter to his fifteen-year-old self. You can read it here:

theplayerstribune.com/articles/2016-6-9-mario-andretti-racing-letter-to-my-younger-self.

The letter is long, over five thousand words. In it, Andretti focuses on the traumatic decision to move to America. He recounts in detail how his life proceeded, including both high and low points. The time he crashed out of a race on the first lap. The serious injuries his twin brother sustained in a wreck. The death of a good friend in a fire. Most of all, he writes about the uncertainty weighing his younger self down with anxiety.

Andretti is able to be so specific because he lived through it. But imagine if you could write a similar letter to your current self from the vantage point of your future self now. Imagine how it would propel you forward with a bias for action. It would mitigate anxiety and paralysis by replacing the fear of failure with the fear of regret, of the chances not taken.

HOW-TO 6: Have your future self write to your present self. When you have a life decision to make, inhabit your future self, who is on the far side of the decision. Then have that future self write a letter to its younger self—that is you, now. Try to make the letter as specific as possible so you can picture how your life unfolds on the other side of the decision.

Three Time Horizons

The general rule is, bigger decisions tend to require a greater distance in time. When it comes to how far in the future we project ourselves, we recommend considering three time horizons: a day, a year, or a decade (or end of life). Give or take. We'll call these near future, mid-future, and far future. The details will vary, but this provides a starting point for picking an optimum time frame given the situation.

Near future

Sometimes all we need is to cast ourselves a short time into the future, with the sole purpose of getting us out of the now. The near-future time frame is an accessible aid for self-control. A day is convenient, although sometimes an hour or less is enough to get us out of the moment. The near future is an ideal place for considering tactical decisions like whether to send a text or email, stay out after midnight on a weekday, or accept the first quote for an order.

HOW-TO 7: Become your near-future self for tactical decisions. This approach can be highly effective for in-the-moment decisions that will have immediate consequences or payoffs. Consider, How much will this matter to me tomorrow? How will I feel about this in an hour? or How important is it to respond to this right now?

For example, an Alzheimer's care unit in Northwest Ohio had a problem.[17] The caregivers worked there because they wanted to help those in need. They were compassionate people, but they were also getting burned out. For all their efforts, their patients belittled them, hit them, and forgot who they were. They faced unreasonable demands on their time and felt overworked. Adding insult to injury, they could go across the street to Walmart and get paid as much or more, without having to suffer such abuse. The treatment took an emotional toll, affecting the caregivers' happiness and health and resulting in high turnover.

The unit decided to try something new. When caregivers

found themselves in trying situations with their patients, moments in which they were most vulnerable to frustration and anger, they paused and imagined how they would feel about the situation in thirty minutes. Now, that is not a particularly long period of time. But it was enough temporal distance to imagine that the acute feelings they had then and there would have passed and reframe how they thought about what happened in the present.

Erin Azar aka Mrs. Space Cadet (@ImMrsSpaceCadet on Instagram) is a self-described "pro struggle runner" who is adept at pairing lighthearted comic relief with wisdom and inspiration. She taps into her near-future self to get herself out for a run when she's otherwise, well, struggling. She calls it "play it forward": "Fast forward one hour and compare how you will feel if you didn't get out for the run with how you'd feel if you did get out for the run (or whatever it was you didn't feel like doing). This works for me 100% of the time."[18]

This near-future perspective helps prioritize our health and relationships, inoculating ourselves against temporary temptations and the manipulations of others. "Would you like to supersize that value meal?" Becoming our future self a mere hour from now, the answer is likely no. Feeling like scrolling social media more than doing an unpleasant task? Become your end-of-the-workday self. What would you have wanted your in-the-moment self to do? What about the donuts or leftover pizza in the break room? Easier to resist if you just become the version of you that is stepping on the scale the next morning. Kids, spouse, or parents do something that drives you crazy? Time travel two hours into the future. (Or maybe you need a full day for this one!) How do you wish you had handled the situation? If nothing else, you can see that what felt so urgent is no longer so, and a response that is effective in the long run always beats a hot in-the-moment reaction. This act of gaining even a small temporal distance, becoming a near-future version of ourselves, separates us from our immersed self and can have a powerful impact.

Mid-future

A midterm time frame is nominally a year into the future, although it could be six months or two years depending on what makes the most sense to you. This might be driven by a seasonal or business cycle. The point is to kick the time frame out of the immediate future and into a space where the impact of the decision will have a chance to unfold. This helps us shed the short-term concerns about practicality or convenience in favor of loftier ideals and values. But we are not talking about a totally different phase of life. Our life and working situation will be much like it is now.

Anett John from the University of Birmingham and Kate Orkin from the University of Oxford studied the effects of visualizing your future self on 3,750 women in Kenya.[19] Contaminated water had been a major problem for Kenyan communities, leading to diarrhea in children that resulted in dehydration and death. In fact, this problem is far from isolated to Kenya; as of 2024, diarrhea is the third-leading cause of death globally for kids under the age of five, killing almost half a million children per year.[20]

Chlorinated water, a highly effective solution, was made available in Kenya, but when John and Orkin began their research, it was infrequently taken advantage of, with just 3 percent of households in their study drinking it. They asked the women to consider their future selves, and their future families, one year out: "Close your eyes for one minute. Imagine the person you will be in one year. Imagine your family in one year." The future-self visualization exercise increased the use of chlorinated tablets 22 percent more than a planning exercise, showing that midterm temporal distancing was more effective than what some would consider a more concrete approach (planning).

For operational decisions, a temporal distance of six months into the future is a sweet spot. When David was a submarine captain on the *Santa Fe*, he would approve which officer was going to drive the submarine into port. A modern submarine's design is optimized for underwater operations. Port entrances are infrequent, and many of these entries are in new places, where no one may have the institutional memory. In addition, a good number of them are evaluated (oh, the stress!). If the goal were just to get the highest score, he would pick the officer best at driving on the surface. Every time that decision came up, he would use the same officer. But eventually, that officer would transfer, and there would be a severe degradation in performance.

With that in mind, he asked himself, Who would my six-month-from-now future self wish we'd used today to drive into port? The question allowed him to see clearly the value of rotating officers and training a deep bench. As a result, the *Santa Fe* outperformed the other subs over time and graduated a disproportionate number of future submarine captains. This is an example of capability development with the help of a temporally distanced coach, tapping into a growth mindset at the organizational level.

This midterm time horizon is good for decisions that are bigger than when you need help not overreacting to something but smaller than changing jobs or developing a new product. To gain the needed distanced-self perspective, with the correct temporal proximity (our relation in time to the decision, situation, or event), consider a time frame somewhere between six months and two years. Think about different options and their likely outcomes, weighted by the probability of each if you're so inclined. The more you do this for yourself, the more you can help others with their decisions as well. Ask what they wish they would have done now if it was already six months hence.

A client told David the following story: She was a senior executive in a premier law enforcement organization. She had an ineffective subordinate who would not respond to emails, would not make decisions, and would not engage with their fellow team members in a useful way. Coworkers who depended on this person's input had developed a work-around: bypass the ineffective employee and ask the boss; so our client was receiving an increasing number of requests for information, clarity, guidance, and approval. This was frustrating. At the same time, many of these requests had fast-moving law enforcement impacts.

The client admitted that she was part of the problem because she would answer these questions. She prioritized getting the immediate work done. By inadvertently rewarding those making the requests, she incentivized their behavior. She was becoming increasingly overloaded and sucked into decisions beneath her pay grade.

This is a good opportunity to apply the midterm time horizon. If she were to imagine herself as her future self one year from now, she would see that she was continuing to answer more and more of these questions without solving the problem. Even though not responding would delay the work today, it would improve workflow in the future if she just enforced the responsibilities expected of her subordinate and elected not to answer any more emails.

Sometimes it's best to start by looking backward and then flipping the perspective. For example, when we would run a retrospective on a recently completed operation, we might ask ourselves,

What do we wish we'd started doing six months ago? and that could spark ideas about what the team ought to start doing now to prepare us better for six months from now. If you want a resilient, independently minded team in the future, what do you need to be doing now to develop those skills and behaviors?

HOW-TO 8: Become your mid-future self for operational decisions. In reviews with your team, try a temporally distanced perspective. You can frame it in the following ways:

- ▶ "What would my one-year-from-now self want *me* to do now?"

- ▶ "If we were to do this again, what do we wish we knew that we didn't know this time?"

- ▶ "If we were to do this again, what do we wish we did that we didn't do this time?"

- ▶ "If another team were to do this in six months, what would we suggest they do differently?"

Far future

The long-term time horizon is meant for any temporal distance from around ten years to the end of life. If you're in the first quarter of your life, you might find five years to be more relatable. In other scenarios, we might pick twenty years or some other number, perhaps for retirement planning. This long-term temporal distancing has powerful effects on adaptive coping with painful experiences, financial health, major life decisions, and overall wisdom. The far-future self is the ideal self and allows us to reframe our perceptions of risk to align with how we more truly wish to live our life. We move to the far side of the decision and replace fear of failure with fear of not trying. Use the far future to be a better human.

Former FBI hostage and crisis negotiator Chris Voss has had to negotiate with some of the worst terrorists and kidnappers on the planet. In an interview on the *Lex Fridman Podcast*,[21] Voss explained his approach throughout his career, using temporal distancing to coach both himself and the person on the other side of the table. He would say, "Imagine that ten years from now, we're both in fantastic positions. . . . We're both happy. . . . Now, let's work our way back from there." He relied on temporal distancing to break out of the detail-oriented and contentious *how* thinking to see the bigger picture in terms of *what* the broader purpose is and *why*, allowing greater flexibility in finding a more mutually agreeable path forward.

Researchers Emma Bruehlman-Senecal and Özlem Ayduk (2015) from the University of California, Berkeley, investigated the effects of temporal distance on coping with emotionally difficult situations by asking people to think about how they might feel in ten years versus a week from now.[22] To help participants make that future seem more real to them, they were asked to "imagine what their life would be like either one week or ten years in the future, envisioning what they 'might be doing' and how they 'might be spending their time.'" When they used the ten-year frame, they felt less distress. It didn't matter whether the distressful event was still going on or whether it was as small as a work deadline or as large as the loss of a spouse.

Emotionally, the ten-year frame results in less negative feelings. Cognitively, it sparks more thinking about ideals for the future and the impermanence of the current situation, less thinking about how the current situation impacts day-to-day life, and less need to avoid thinking about the situation. The researchers also studied how students reacted to midterm exam scores and found that for those who got low scores, the ten-years-in-the-future condition resulted in less distress than when participants just focused generically on "in the future," or when they were allowed to reflect on the negative event in any way they found helpful. When something bothers us beyond a fleeting flash of emotions, perhaps because it actually has consequences for our future, projecting ourselves in a distant future, such as ten years from now, and then looking back at it, allows us to process the event more effectively and helps us experience less distress.

This approach helps us shed or better process our emotional baggage. It helps us discard our biases. It changes the nature of our fear of regret: We shift from fear of action to fear of inaction. We accept the risk of failure and become more concerned about the risk of not trying.

The far future can extend to an end-of-life time horizon and beyond. Becoming our end-of-life self is best for considering big-picture changes. An even further distanced, more abstract, higher-level perspective is thinking beyond the end of your life. For example, are you leaving an inheritance for your family, creating a legacy, or fostering environmental sustainability?

Stephen Covey is known for his mantra, "Begin with the end in mind." One of the activities he recommends in *The 7 Habits of Highly Effective People* is to write your own epitaph.[23] He also invites us to imagine our own funeral, with people talking about us from four dimensions of our lives: family, friends, work, and community. What will they say? What would you want them to say?

When Joe Biden stepped aside as the Democratic candidate for president of the United States, Arthur Brooks used the example to write about the importance of crafting the end of our story, not just the beginning.[24] Brooks teaches courses on leadership and happiness at Harvard Business School, but this is a topic of personal importance to him.

Brooks served as the president of the American Enterprise Institute from 2009 to 2019. Toward the end of his tenure, he sought a trusted friend's advice on when to step down. The answer he got was, "You either leave when you still have more to offer or you can leave on someone else's terms." He says he chose to leave "a little before [he] was ready." Annie Duke echoes this: "Quitting at the right time feels like we are quitting early."[25]

To be clear, we are not advocating that everyone quit what they are doing now or even quit early. What we are saying is that for high-stakes decisions with long-term implications, such as whether to stay or leave a current position or career, we need to adopt a far-future perspective. How do we want to end our story?

Spoiler alert: Our far-future self often wants us to focus on improving our relationships. For more than eighty-five years, the Harvard Study of Adult Development has found one thing that continually comes up as important for healthy, happy, long lives: good relationships.[26]

HOW-TO 9: Become your far-future self to be a better person. If you're on the youthful side of seventy, try using eighty years old or your end-of-life self. Imagine you really are that person. Where are you now? What is important to you? What is your life like? What are you doing? Inhabit that future version of you. Become that person. Now look back on your current situation. From your new perspective, reflect on the issue or decision your former self was facing. Remember, that person is someone else now. What should [your name] do? What do you wish they would choose? What advice do you have for them? Another tool you can use is to start in the far off, distant future and then shorten the time horizon. This is useful if you are trying to spur action toward a future objective. In *Dopamine Nation*, Anna Lembke is talking to a client who is a habitual cannabis user but wants to quit.[27] The interaction goes like this:

"Do you think you would be able and willing to stop cannabis for a month?"

"Hmmm . . . I don't think I'm ready to try quitting now, but maybe later. For sure I'm not going to be smoking like this forever."

"Do you still want to be using cannabis like this ten years from now?"

"No. No way. Definitely not." She shook her head vigorously.

"How about five years from now?"

"No, not in five years either."

"How about a year from now?"

Pause. Chuckle. "I guess you got me there, Doc. If I don't want to be using like this in a year, I might as well try to stop now."

She looked at me and smiled. "Okay, let's do this."

While we may imagine ourselves far in the future, the action we take is now.

We spoke with an executive coach in Phoenix who advises his clients to maintain an imaginary plus-twenty-year-old avatar of themselves. As they age, the avatar ages, always staying twenty years older. When they come to significant life decisions, they inhabit their plus-twenty-year-old self, consider the situation, and use that perspective to make the decision.

HOW-TO 10: Start long, then reel it in. For major change, become your far-future self and imagine how you want to be at that point, then roll back to shorter time frames. This is a good approach when it comes to stopping unhealthy habits or starting healthy ones.

How to Be Your Future Self

1. **Fast-forward to the far side.** Imagine you've already made the decision. Instead of thinking of the decision as being before you, think of it as already having happened. How did it turn out? Now what would you choose?

2. **Become pen pals with your future self.** In your letter, describe the issue at hand or the decision you need to make. And then respond to your present self as your future self. What does your future self say?

3. **Project yourself into the future.** What is your life like? Describe this in vivid detail.

4. **Act now, not in the future.** As much as possible, perform any actions on behalf of your future self now. Create a default for the desired action.

5. **Think backward.** What were you like ten years ago? Consider how much you've changed since then. Now think about how much you could change in the next ten years.

6. **Have your future self write to your present self.** Inhabit your future self and write to your current self from the far side of a decision.

7. **Become your near-future self for tactical decisions.** Do this as an emotional stopgap or as a way to exert self-control. Project yourself thirty minutes to a day in the future.

8. **Become your mid-future self for operational decisions.** For operational decisions or routine opportunities for growth, project yourself six months to two years into the future.

9. **Become your far-future self to be a better person.** Get the long-term perspective on any ongoing situation, whether ten years out or even further.

10. **Start long, then reel it in.** For difficult decisions about changing bad habits, start with a desired far-future state. Then work backward.

Summary

Roman emperor and philosopher Marcus Aurelius wrote in what would become his *Meditations*, "Think of yourself as dead. You have lived your life. Now take what's left and live it properly."[28] Though this may be the ultimate time horizon from which to view yourself, the basic concept can be applied to the short-term and the midterm as well. Time traveling to become our future self achieves three things: It moves us closer to our end of life, putting us on the far side of any major decision and triggering a regret framework; it highlights what is desirable to be our ideal and true self over what is merely practical; and it mitigates self-control failure. Temporal distancing is a powerful decision aid. We challenge you to become your future self and tell your hospice nurse what it is that you will regret not doing. Then return from that journey and start living that life now.

8

Stop Time

*The right word may be effective, but no word was
ever as effective as a rightly timed pause.*

—MARK TWAIN

Shane Mac is a high-energy serial entrepreneur, business founder, and CEO. Ten minutes after speaking with him, he'll send you an email with links to any articles or resources you had been talking about and connect you with anyone he knows who had come up in your discussion. Every time. He's thoughtful, listens intently, and is intensely curious. Fortunately for us, he is also willing to be vulnerable and share his failures.

Shane is currently building XMTP, a decentralized messaging protocol. Before this, he built a different messaging platform that was a major partner with Facebook, Apple, Google, and Whats-App. After raising more capital, a major partner was considering an acquisition that would put the company into the next tier: $50 million or more. It wasn't just a partnership; it would have been a home run.

Shane had spent five months building a relationship with the potential partner's chief technology officer (CTO), and it seemed like everything was on track. They shared inspiring texts about the future with each other, along with personal stories about their families. They had established a sense of trust and goodwill, and in Shane's mind, a resilient relationship. Then, all of a sudden, in Shane's words, "The partnership went from great to break, and fast."

Shane's team started blaming their partner's team for issues related to the upcoming launch, and vice versa. Shane and the CTO tried to manage the complaints and reinforce trust in the partnership, telling their respective teams to just focus on their side of the project. But eventually, Shane began feeling increasingly drawn into his team's emotional state, agreeing with them about their "inept counterparts" on the other team. Self-immersed, they tumbled headlong into overclaiming and self-serving biases and blame, breeding resentment. Shane was immersed in his team's identity and in his own.

It all came to a head one day. Shane sent an accusatory text to the CTO. Ten minutes later, he heard a ping—his excitement and fear both growing. He stopped what he was doing, grabbed his phone, and read the following message from the CTO:

I'll be blunt. I'm not very much digging the blame vibe from your team. Like VERY much not. All the professing "we" doesn't erase the language I'm seeing from you and your team. Expletives, arrogance claims, referring to platforms and people as "shit." It's just not cool. I've been nothing but admitting our faults, and they are plenty. I've referred to them specifically and talked to ways we're addressing them.

Shane shares, "I channeled all the frustrations my team had shared with me over months directly through my fingertips to let him know how I felt. I'll never forget that moment. It's almost like you black out in the moment and end up in a typing deleting typing deleting typing edit deleting type type type delete copy paste delete trance." It's a feeling we've all experienced. He blasted back:

> I'll be blunt. I'm not very much digging the blame vibe from you and your team. Like VERY much not. All the professing "we" doesn't erase the language I'm seeing from you and your team. Expletives, arrogance claims, referring to platforms and people as "shit." It's just not cool. This was the most painful partnership we've ever done. . . .

Shane was stuck in self-immersion, locked into seeing the world from his perspective, and prompted to an immediacy of action and reaction that was unnecessary. Some might say he was "triggered." The word implies an impulsive reaction we're not in control of, a loss of "response-ability," the ability to choose our response. Shane needed a circuit breaker, something to interrupt the impulsive back-and-forth. He needed to distance.

It felt *so* gratifying when Shane sent his snarky text response back. Take that! Shane successfully vindicated his me-here-and-now self. But we bet that you can predict what happened next.

It killed the deal. He now says, "That was the text that cost me and our investors $50 million." But it was also a lesson—an expensive one—that has stuck with him ever since. Being locked in your own head can cost you big-time—relationships, money, business opportunities. An inability to pause, step out, and consider the potential ramifications creates a situation in which you are bound to lose. The problem is, once we start descending into an immersed state, our ability to override our impulses and call a time-out on ourselves is, itself, impaired.

Value of a Pause

To see a counterexample, just look at how Steve Jobs handled a hostile question at the 1997 Worldwide Developers Conference. An audience member literally maligned his competence, saying, "It's sad and clear that at several counts you don't know what you're talking about," before asking a technical question. How did Jobs respond? He sat down, took a sip of water, and paused—for a full ten seconds. He defused the situation with humor and humility before giving a real answer. He dignified the questioner as well as himself. What was he doing during those ten seconds? He was taking a distanced perspective in order to coach himself on how best to respond.

Remember when Anne Hathaway interrupted the filming of *Les Misérables*? She called a pause and proceeded to talk to herself in the third person. Then she belted out "I Dreamed a Dream" and nailed it. She won numerous awards for her performance, including an Academy Award and Golden Globe for best supporting actress. Her process reveals four key steps for calling a pause and using psychological distance when it matters.

The first step is to make the pause possible. When the culture, setup, and momentum is built up around not calling a pause, it feels nearly impossible to do so. Here's something Anne Hathaway did that neither Captain Lee nor Shane Mac did. A week before her shoot, she went to the director, Tom Hooper, and confessed she was feeling nervous about singing "I Dreamed a Dream." Hathaway acknowledged her anxiety up front, so it was not a taboo she felt she needed to hide. This acknowledgment laid the groundwork, preparing herself and others to do what it would take to make sure she could be dialed in when she needed to be.

When Hathaway did this, it moved this fear from "hidden" to

"known to self and known to others" in the Johari Window. This is in contrast to Captain Lee, who kept his anxiety about landing without the electronic glideslope to himself.

Second, Hathaway recognized the need to call a pause. The situational wrinkle she had to contend with was that the director wanted the actors to do their own singing while being filmed and, even more challenging, during a single take. This approach gave the film the feel of a live Broadway performance, but it also meant the actors did not have the safety net of studio retakes or voice-overs during the in-scene performance. Hathaway saw ahead of time that this situation would be high pressure and would likely make her feel self-conscious.

Then, in the moment of performance, Hathaway could tell she was in the wrong frame of mind: "I couldn't stop thinking about how if I messed it up how exposed I would feel." She—and probably everyone else watching—could tell that her first takes were off. But it was her awareness that she was not in the right frame of mind, her monitoring of her own thoughts and feelings, that clued her in on the need to call a pause. She describes in her own words, "I was so angry with myself"—an indication to mentally regroup.

Third, Hathaway did what is obvious by now to you and us but was neither obvious to Shane in the moment nor to Captain Lee as he approached the landing. Using clear language that she knew and that others around her understood, she called a pause. A time-out. "No, no. Stop. I'm sorry. The balance, it's off." Calling a pause is a necessary precondition for using the distancing tools to reframe effectively.

Fourth, having called a pause, Hathaway's next step was to exit self-immersion and distance along one of the dimensions to gain the necessary perspective to attack the problem. She chose illeism: becoming someone else, becoming her own coach. "I closed my eyes and I remember thinking, 'Hathaway, if you do not do this in this moment, you have no right to call yourself an actor. Put aside all that bulls— and just do your job.' I opened my eyes and I'm like [snaps fingers]: 'Let's go.' And I did it. That was the one that I let rip, and that was the one that was in the piece."

Let's explore each of these four steps for calling a pause when we need psychological distance:

1. Make the pause possible.

2. Recognize the situation.

3. Call the pause.

4. Decide your distancing dimension.

Make the Pause Possible

Making the pause possible requires prep work. The objective of the prep work is to reduce any social or cultural barriers to calling a pause, so doing so becomes easy, expected, and normal. When Hathaway realized this scene for *Les Misérables* was going to be a challenge for her, she brought it to the attention of the director. Laying groundwork to call a pause readies us to do so when we need it. This is important because we usually don't know in advance precisely when we will need to call a pause. Normalizing a break in the action as being a natural part of the task at hand allows us to engage a pause while staying task focused and not veering into image management. It can be helpful to have an up-front conversation about pausing if needed. Hathaway had told her director she was nervous about the part; so, her calling a pause was not unexpected. Military personnel have specific phrases and hand signals for calling a pause. Game referees and coaches have a protocol and designated signal for pausing the action and calling time-out. This shared understanding of how calling a pause is actually task focused makes it easier to execute and take subsequent actions that might otherwise risk our image and threaten our perceived competence. For example, referees can rewind the tape to review a play or a call. This is task-focused behavior.

Captain Lee made a different choice when learning about the situational wrinkle he felt unprepared to contend with: avoidance. We saw how well that worked. Making the pause possible is responsible, ethical, and is ingrained in the highest-performing teams and organizations.

A good example of a mechanism that makes a pause possible is the "andon cord," a concept that originated in Takaoka, Japan, where the Toyota Corolla was produced. It was a simple cord that, when pulled, activated a lantern above the assembly line, indicating the worker at that position had a problem.

Pulling the cord of this *andon*—the Japanese word for "paper lantern"—would stop the assembly line if the problem wasn't quickly resolved. It signaled a pause. But the power of the andon cord was not just in calling the pause, nor even the stoppage of the assembly line. Rather, the core underlying change that the andon cord symbolized was the acceptance of and expressed gratitude for calling a pause. The cord was a visible artifact of appreciation for the bravery and concern for the products' and the workers' welfare required to bring production to a grinding halt over the mere possibility that something might be amiss. There is usually some degree of risk in calling time-out. We've all experienced moments of uncertainty in which we're unsure whether the right thing to do is raise our hand—or pull the cord—and interrupt the action. The price is potential embarrassment on a personal level, for the potential benefit of the organization. The near-universal use of the word *wrong* is a barrier to speaking and making these interruptions. People use the term to describe a pause that turns out to have been unnecessary. The consequence is that people need to convince themselves of a high level of certainty that the issue they are questioning is authentic before speaking up. Not describing pauses as wrong, but rather as acts of resilience, and the practice of stating probabilities when explaining why they are being called are two linguistic steps that ease the path toward calling a pause. If we are uncertain whether there is a problem, we certainly need to call a pause.

David sat next to a football video replay referee on the Acela train from Washington, DC, to New York City. Knowing that a referee has little time to decide whether to interrupt play or to let it continue, he was interested in how they decide whether or not to stop the game in order to check the video. The referee said that if they cannot call it clean, then play is paused. They have made the pause the norm, placing burden of proof on the continuation of play.

HOW-TO 1: Make the pause possible. Make the importance of the pause clear to your team. Build it into your culture, the way Toyota did with the andon cord. Agree on a signal, a symbol, or language that will enable team members to call a pause when necessary, without fear. This is why sports coaches and referees have a whistle and the game clock. Normalize calling the pause by modeling this behavior to all. Practice it until it's no big deal.

Recognize the Situation

In the conclusion of *Thinking, Fast and Slow*,[1] Nobel Prize–winning psychologist Daniel Kahneman, who spent his prolific career studying human cognitive biases and decision errors, reflects on his personal journey to overcome his own natural human biases. He makes a startling admission: For all his efforts and study, he finds he is not much better at undoing his cognitive biases. But he has improved in his ability to recognize the types of situations that are most likely to warp his thinking.

We help ourselves most by learning to recognize when a situation is likely to result in suboptimal cognitive performance, biases, or decision errors. We can prepare ahead of time for situations that are likely to push us into a self-immersed state, necessitating a pause to initiate the exit from self-immersion. Four common situational factors that drive self-immersion are urgency, live performance or in public, feedback, and reliving painful past experiences.

Urgency

Urgency creates stress, and stress is likely to deepen our state of immersion. From there, our focus is hijacked from task to self without us even realizing it. Defensiveness and self-protection take over, and our minds engage to curate a reality that makes us feel good about ourselves. Life often comes at us with a sense of immediacy. But sometimes the urgency is contrived or self-induced, in which case gaining psychological distance can help us place the apparent urgency in a broader context. For example, an internal production deadline might need to be moved so we can make a better product or decision.

Live Performance or in Public

With any type of performance, especially those done live in public, there exists a strong natural tendency to feel self-conscious or anxious. While anxiety can be either a benefit or a liability, self-consciousness is detrimental because it hijacks cognitive attention away from the task itself. Self-distancing allows us to channel anxiety in a positive direction, helping us rise to the challenge, while decreasing self-consciousness.

Feedback

"Can I give you some advice?" According to neuroscientist David Rock, this question is the "cortisol equivalent of hearing footsteps [behind you] in the dark."[2] Seeking out your own problems, deficiencies, or areas for improvement is not always an appealing endeavor. And when thrust upon you, feedback can feel quite threatening. This applies to informally volunteered feedback, as well as postmortem reviews and formal evaluations. Kudos to those who embrace feedback. For those who struggle with wanting to receive brutal honesty on your performance, behavior, or actions, distancing helps it not be about you.

Painful Past Experiences

We are flawed humans. We make mistakes. And there is no escaping loss. Other times, we are the victims of the bad behavior of others. We are not advocating the use of self-distancing to avoid the raw experience of pain. That would be dysfunctional; pain is a necessary part of life. But at some point, we need to accept what has happened and move on. When we are ruminating on a painful or negative experience—reliving it over and over again—this is a cue that distance is needed to reframe or reappraise the situation. The distanced perspective will help us accept, grow, and move forward with our lives.

HOW-TO 2: Recognize the situation. Stressful, threatening, or painful situations are likely to prime you for self-immersion, which focuses attention on self-preservation rather than on performance or growth. Notice what situations in your past have triggered this reaction. Write them down and add to this list over time. These red flags will help you anticipate what might cause you to react in the future, so you can be prepared to pause and distance.

Seeing the Red Flags

A painful experience teaches us to avoid a similar situation in the future. After the sting of losing a $50 million deal, Shane Mac takes a much different approach to the moments that could make or break a deal. And not just a business deal, but a relationship or other opportunity. Whether it's a text message, an email, a phone call, or an in-person conversation, Mac has embraced the power of the pause. He asks himself: "Do I have an overwhelming feeling that I *must* send this message?" If the answer is yes, then it's a red flag. The more urgency he feels to send a follow-up text, the more he knows he needs to stop himself and get some much-needed perspective. Mac says, "I have to take an honest look at myself and see if I'm being driven by an urgent feeling to act, or if I feel calm and able to select the right time to send."

Meanwhile, the greater the urgency, the more he needs to check in on how he feels. Is he agitated? Guts churning? Is he twitching, sweating? For him, "the body keeps the score and watching for those signals has become a game changer." But if the voice in his head is saying that he could, for example, send that message later today or tomorrow, after he's polished the language or given it some further thought, he recognizes it would be fine to send at any time. He knows he's not being reactive or driven by fear or ego. "That feeling of calm clarity and having options can't be confused with that frantic urgency."

This new way of thinking has helped keep Mac out of what he calls the "doom loop." That little pause allows him the space to think over what he's actually doing, what he should be doing, and what the consequences may be. His plan is a pre-consideration of his future self. He has a protocol in place to become Coach, step in, and blow the whistle. Call time-out. Pause the action. Chill. Because once we are overly upset or excited, we lose the perspective we need to recognize what is happening and deploy an effective strategy.

Like Shane, we all have tells. We've all been there. A feeling rising up in our body, like water starting to boil. Some heat. A little sweat. Maybe our heart rate kicks up or our muscles contract. We feel adrenaline. That level of intensity is a dead giveaway. There are other indicators: rapid speech, a high-pitched voice, a tightened jaw, shallow breathing, a clenched hand or foot.

Though these tells may vary from person to person, they are all physical responses to an imminent threat. When your body is saying you have to do something right now, you feel like *now* is all that matters. An overwhelming sense that *everything is now*.

But unless you are literally about to get hit by a bus, that sudden urgency is contrived and will serve you poorly. Like a toxin that anesthetizes us to its effects, false urgency takes our cerebral cortex offline and convinces us that we are thinking clearly when we are not. By identifying our own tells, we can more readily become Coach, call time-out, and give ourselves the chance to calm down and regroup.

HOW-TO 3: Recognize your tells. What happens before you feel the urge to act rashly or to defend yourself? What are you experiencing in your body? What emotions are swirling through you? What are you thinking? Pay attention and take note of your tells when you become self-immersed. These are the times you want to call a pause. Practice looking for them ahead of time so you're prepared. Otherwise, when the moment strikes, it'll be too late.

Call the Pause

Once we have made a pause possible and recognized the need to call a pause, the actual calling is a relatively simple matter. Say, "I need a moment," "Let's take a five-minute break and regroup," or "Time-out." Or use the agreed-upon signal or symbol. This may be blowing a whistle, making a hand gesture, or pulling a cord. If you don't have one preplanned, just say, "Pause."

Sometimes we can call a pause to halt the action right in the moment. But other times we need to rely on a naturally occurring pause. William Ury imagined being on the balcony during breaks in the negotiation. He had to be present and listening during the moments of conversation. Jeremy Snape and his team became Balcony Boy between batters. Simone Biles coached herself in between events.

Brief interruptions serve a similar function as naturally occurring pauses, facilitating decision-making by increasing psychological distance.[3] When we experience an interruption, it creates a momentary cognitive break that distances us from the task at hand. This distance shifts our thinking from low construal to high construal. Greater psychological distance also leads to decisions based more on desirability than on feasibility when relevant trade-offs are considered. For example, selecting a restaurant based on your favorite cuisine rather than on convenience, or reconsidering a purchase just because it's a great deal.

Interruptions can act as a form of pause, allowing us to step away and see the bigger picture instead of getting bogged down in the details. The study of interruptions supports the value of calling a pause during decision-making. Just as a brief interruption can enhance abstract thinking, pausing allows leaders to step away from the immediate demands of a situation and engage in more thoughtful, deliberate decision-making. The pause creates the psychological distance necessary to transition from reactive, emotionally charged decisions to more strategic, long-term ones. This insight underlines the importance of calling a pause, not just as a tactical break, but as a cognitive tool that shifts our mindset toward clarity and better leadership.

HOW-TO 4: Come up with language, a signal, or symbol. Meet with your team and agree on how you'd like to express the need for a pause. Use this consistently. Call a pause when necessary.

In 2023, Edwin Castro won the largest Powerball payout to date, $2.04 billion, after buying three $2 tickets. He opted for a lump-sum payout and, after taxes, walked away with $628.5 million. That's a massive amount. Invested at 5 percent, it would spin off over $30 million a year. What did Castro do with the money? Well, he vacationed in Fiji and bought some really fast (and expensive) cars and three mansions—one for $25 million, one for $47 million, and one for $4 million (OK, that was for his parents). In an article in *Fortune* magazine, Paul Karger, a financial adviser to centimillionaires and billionaires, says he should "just chill. Don't make any major decisions or big commitments. Let things digest."[4] In other words, call a pause.

Decide Your Distancing Dimension

We have covered three distancing dimensions: be someone else, be somewhere else, and be sometime else. They are linked and mutually reinforcing. Being sometime else supports being somewhere else, and both invite a sense of being someone else. All the distancing dimensions have a similar effect on our construal level, perspective, and decision-making capabilities. However, certain dimensions might be a more natural fit for certain situations.

We can infer from the types of scenarios that the researchers use which one might be a better option under which conditions. In the stressful situation for Hathaway, it was to be someone else. In the decision crucible for Moore and Grove, it was also to be someone else—their replacements. Spatial distancing, on the other hand, helps with decision-making in situations of information overload. It has a visual element to it and has also proved helpful in challenging situations where mentally projecting ourselves somewhere else—a balcony, a higher floor, the top of a mountain, outer space—helps us gain perspective of the big picture. If the situation or decision comes with a strong sense of urgency, then temporal distancing might be the way to go. Clear your mind and avoid regret by projecting yourself into the near-, mid-, or far-future time horizon, and then look back on the decision. Become Morning Guy. Write your obituary.

The purpose of calling a pause is not solely to take a break. We call a pause to give ourselves the space to pick the next play. We disengage to decide which distancing dimension to use to gain the necessary perspective that is right for the situation or decision. Then we pick a technique: illeism, being on the balcony, zooming out, becoming our future self. We become Coach. We advise ourselves. Then we go back into the moment and execute.

HOW-TO 5: Pick your play. Choose your distancing dimension: Be someone else, be somewhere else, or be sometime else.

How to Stop Time

1. **Make the pause possible.** Build the pause into your culture. Normalize calling the pause by modeling this behavior to your team and organization.

2. **Recognize the situation.** Take note of stressful situations in the past that have triggered self-immersion. Add to this list over time.

3. **Recognize your tells.** Tune in to the physical and emotional indicators that make you want to defend yourself. This will help you anticipate when Coach should call a time-out, giving you the chance to take a step back, disengage, and then reengage with the situation at hand.

4. **Come up with language, a signal, or symbol.** Use the agreed-upon expression to call a pause. It could be as simple as saying, "I need a pause."

5. **Pick your play.** Choose your distancing dimension: self, spatial, or temporal.

Summary

Whether it's a $50 million text or a conversation with a team member that goes awry, sometimes the best thing to do is to pause. Blow the whistle for a time-out and become Coach. Then implement one of the self-, spatial-, or temporal-distancing techniques. Pick your favorite or whichever is best suited to the situation. Any of the tools will be better than none of them. But of course, all of this is predicated on our ability to call a pause in the first place, which itself requires that we get some practice identifying the types of situations or conditions that push us into self-immersion in the first place. Since immersion is our default state, we must deliberately choose a distanced perspective. To do that, we need to pause the action first. Knowing *when* to call a time-out is therefore just as crucial as knowing how to distance.

CONCLUSION

*Indeed, I find that distance lends perspective and I
often write better of a place when I am some distance
from it. One can be so overwhelmed by the forest
as to miss seeing the trees.*

—LOUIS L'AMOUR,
EDUCATION OF A WANDERING MAN

Be someone else. Be somewhere else. Be sometime else.

When we step outside ourselves to create distance, our viewpoint changes instantly. The radical difference in our ability to see reality and ourselves more clearly with this simple mental manipulation is uncanny. We become our own coach through this new vantage point, and then we coach ourselves from there. Becoming someone else grants us the fresh and unbiased eyes of an impartial observer. We shed the dysfunctional effects of ego that manifest when we are stuck in self-immersion. Be someone else in situations where we have too much of our identity at stake or when we are stuck ruminating about a past event.

When we mentally relocate, our new visual vantage point provides a broader context, so we're able to see the big picture. We see the gestalt. We are able to focus on what is important without being distracted by the details. We also see ourselves as a mere part of the action, just like everyone else. Our pumped-up self-importance deflates. Be somewhere else in situations where you have information overload, are hung up on particular details, or are concerned about your own image.

When we time travel to the future and look back, we naturally reframe decisions in terms of regret and lost opportunities, as opposed to threat and change, which invites us to live bigger lives. Be sometime else when the inertia of comfort with the status quo overpowers thoughts of change, when risk aversion is rampant, when planning for the future, and when making big life decisions.

Self-distancing by being someone else, somewhere else, or sometime else elevates our thinking. We focus on a higher purpose and meaning as opposed to the tedious details of execution. We consider strategic *what*, *why*, and *whether* questions, instead of being stuck in tactical *how* questions. We are our truer selves, aligning our actions with our values and seeing through the excuses of convenience and practicality. We become closer to our ideal selves and aspire to be better humans.

Once we understand these three distancing dimensions and practice the various techniques, we recognize that they do not exist separately. These three dimensions are interconnected and reinforce one another: We cannot, for example, relocate ourselves mentally without feeling, at least to some degree, that we have become a different person. Further, baked into the notion of traveling through time is the idea that we are no longer viewing the world from our own perspective but are looking back at ourselves from another's. There's a reason George Lucas opened Star Wars with, "A long time ago in a galaxy far, far away" and not "Not so long ago in a galaxy nearby"—he wanted to transport the audience to a whole new world. Our brains link these dimensions together; far away in space feels like far away in time, and far away in time feels like far away in space.

These dimensions work in concert to help us achieve Coach's

perspective, and imagining ourselves as Coach can activate all three at once. In time and with practice, we can more easily exit self-immersion and achieve a distanced state, creating the necessary space to see clearly and make better decisions.

To become Coach, it may be helpful to affirm in your mind an image of this separate persona that you become instead of you. Coach has our best interests at heart and wants us to win but remains calm and objective. Coach is supportive but honest. Coach encourages us toward our goals but also tells us what we need to hear. Coach sees us as simply part of a team and an even smaller part of a bigger context. Coach's outside-in, observer perspective means we are not mired in defending and justifying why we ran the last play the way we did. We leave behind what no longer serves us. No matter what happens, Coach is always trying to figure out what to do next. Coach is focused on moving forward. As Coach, we learn more, perform better, and make wiser decisions for ourselves, our teams, and our organizations. Better yet, we can help others do the same.

ACKNOWLEDGMENTS

We are grateful to the experts, supporters, storytellers, and critics who helped shape the ideas for this book and brought clarity and order to our vision of a helpful decision-making guide for leaders and anyone wanting to live a fuller life.

We would like to thank the team at Portfolio/Penguin Random House, including Adrian Zackheim, who believed in the project, and our editor, Casey Ebro, who diligently went through many iterations of the manuscript.

We would especially like to thank those who shared stories of their experiences with distancing—or not—and the resulting outcomes, including Bob Reeves, Brenton Ford, Burak Alici, Ethan Kross, Gareth Holebrook, George Kohlrieser, Jan Hagen, Jennifer Gillespie, Jennifer Pierce, Jeremy Snape, Jim Dryburgh, Kim Harrison, Maciej Trybulec, Mark Hodges, Peter Russian, Phill Zdybel, Shane Mac, Steve Prevaux, and Thiri Holebrook. They all contributed vital guidance early on, focusing our efforts on the psychological impact of distancing and the power of Coach as a persona.

Mike's students and workshop attendees challenged the way he approached the study of reason and helped him hone some of the examples in this book. David's connections on LinkedIn and his keynote subjects often provided crowdsourced input.

Finally, to our families, who suffered inattention and early mornings so we could push this over the finish line.

NOTES

INTRODUCTION

1. L. David Marquet, *Turn the Ship Around!* (Portfolio, 2013).

2. L. David Marquet, *Leadership Is Language* (Portfolio, 2021).

3. Dizik, Alina, "The Relationship Between Corporate Culture and Performance," *The Wall Street Journal*, February 21, 2016, wsj.com/articles/the -relationship-between-corporate-culture-and-performance-1456110320.

CHAPTER 1: THE IMMERSED SELF

1. National Transportation Safety Board (NTSB), *Descent Below Visual Glidepath and Impact with Seawall Asiana Airlines Flight 214, Boeing 777-200ER, HL7742 San Francisco, California July 6, 2013,* Aircraft Accident Report NTSB/AAR-14/01, Washington, DC, 2014.

2. Mark R. Leary, *The Curse of the Self: Self-Awareness, Egotism, and the Quality of Human Life* (Oxford University Press, 2007).

3. Theo Von, host, *This Past Weekend with Theo Von*, podcast, episode 460, "Jordan Peterson," August 29, 2023, 2:20:03, podcasts.apple.com/us /podcast/jordan-peterson/id1190981360?i=1000626052367.

4. Mark R. Leary, "Motivational and Emotional Aspects of the Self," *Annual Review of Psychology* 58 (January 2007): 317–44, doi.org/10.1146/annurev .psych.58.110405.085658.

5. Jonathan Haidt, *The Righteous Mind: Why Good People Are Divided by Politics and Religion* (Vintage Books, 2012).

6. Daniel Kahneman, *Thinking, Fast and Slow* (Farrar, Straus and Giroux, 2011).

7. Margaret Heffernan, *Willful Blindness: Why We Ignore the Obvious at Our Peril* (Anchor Canada, 2012).

8. Binyamin Cooper et al., "Trapped by a First Hypothesis: How Rudeness Leads to Anchoring," *Journal of Applied Psychology* 107, no. 3 (March 2022): 481–502, doi.org/10.1037/apl0000914.

9. Geoff MacDonald and Mark R. Leary, "Why Does Social Exclusion Hurt? The Relationship Between Social and Physical Pain," *Psychological Bulletin* 131, no. 2 (2005): 202–23, doi.org/10.1037/0033-2909.131.2.202.

10. John Hook, "Affective Neuroscience: Jaak Panksepp's 'Rat Tickling Theory of Emotion,'" *BJPsych Advances* (2024): 1–4, doi.org/10.1192/bja.2023.71.

11. Barbara H. Herman and Jaak Panksepp, "Effects of Morphine and Naloxone on Separation Distress and Approach Attachment: Evidence for Opiate Mediation of Social Affect," *Pharmacology Biochemistry and Behavior* 9, no. 2 (August 1978): 213–20, doi.org/10.1016/0091-3057(78)90167-3.

12. Nathan C. DeWall et al., "Acetaminophen Reduces Social Pain: Behavioral and Neural Evidence," *Psychological Science* 21, no. 7 (2010): 931–37, doi.org/10.1177/0956797610374741.

13. Zhansheng Chen et al., "When Hurt Will Not Heal: Exploring the Capacity to Relive Social and Physical Pain," *Psychological Science* 19, no. 8 (August 2008): 789–95, doi.org/10.1111/j.1467-9280.2008.02158.x.

14. Andrey Anikin et al., "Do Some Languages Sound More Beautiful than Others?" *Proceedings of the National Academy of Sciences of the United States of America* 120, no. 17 (April 17, 2023), doi.org/10.1073/pnas.2218367120.

15. Brad Barber et al., "Learning Fast or Slow?" *SSRN Electronic Journal*, 2014, doi.org/10.2139/ssrn.2535636.

16. Derek Horstmeyer, "When Investors Do the Most Harm with Market Timing," *The Wall Street Journal*, May 5, 2023, wsj.com/articles/investing-market-timing-ad3c230a.

17. Jason Zweig, "Want to Beat the Stock Market? Avoid the Cost of 'Being Human,'" *The Wall Street Journal*, April 14, 2023, wsj.com/articles/active-vs-passive-index-fund-beat-the-stock-market-58e8bd83.

18. Charles Rotblut, "Is the AAII Sentiment Survey a Contrarian Indicator?" *AAII (American Association of Individual Investors) Journal*, June 2013, aaii.com/journal/article/is-the-aaii-sentiment-survey-a-contrarian-indicator.

19. Jason Zweig, "Mirror, Mirror on the Wall, Who Knew That Stocks Would Fall?" *The Wall Street Journal*, December 16, 2022, wsj.com/articles /hindsight-bias-investing-11671206329.

20. Ola Svenson, "Are We All Less Risky and More Skillful Than Our Fellow Drivers?" *Acta Psychologica* 47, no. 2 (February 1981): 143–48, doi.org /10.1016/0001-6918(81)90005-6.

CHAPTER 2: THE DISTANCED SELF

1. Andrew S. Grove and Gordon E. Moore, *1985 Intel Corporation Annual Report*, 1985.

2. Andrew S. Grove, *Only the Paranoid Survive* (Crown Currency, 1999), 88.

3. Grove, *Only the Paranoid Survive*, 89.

4. "Yaacov Trope, Professor of Psychology, Research," New York University, as.nyu.edu/faculty/yaacov-trope.html.

5. Nira Liberman and Yaacov Trope, "The Role of Feasibility and Desirability Considerations in Near and Distant Future Decisions: A Test of Temporal Construal Theory," *Journal of Personality and Social Psychology* 75, no. 1 (1998): 5–18, doi.org/10.1037/0022-3514.75.1.5.

6. Grove, *Only the Paranoid Survive*, 92.

7. Smriti, "What Happened to Digital Equipment Corporation?" *InspireIP* (blog), February 2, 2024, inspireip.com/what-happened-to-digital-equipment -corporation.

8. Atul Gawande, "Personal Best," *The New Yorker*, October 3, 2011, newyorker .com/magazine/2011/10/03/personal-best.

CHAPTER 3: BECOME COACH

1. Francois Brochet et al., "CEO Tenure and Firm Value," *The Accounting Review* 96, no. 6 (November 1, 2021): 47–71, doi.org/10.2308/tar-2019-0295.

2. Emma Goldberg, "The CEOs Who Just Won't Quit: What Happens to a Company—and the Economy—When the Boss Refuses to Retire?" *The New York Times*, May 9, 2024, nytimes.com/2024/05/09/magazine/forever -ceos.html.

3. Donald C. Hambrick and Gregory D. S. Fukutomi, "The Seasons of a CEO's Tenure," *Academy of Management Review* 16, no. 4 (October 1, 1991): 719–42, doi.org/10.5465/amr.1991.4279621.

4. Harper Lee, *To Kill a Mockingbird* (J. B. Lippincott, 1960).

5. Emily Pronin, "How We See Ourselves and How We See Others," *Science* 320, no. 5880 (2008): 1177–80, doi.org/10.1126/science.1154199.

6. Michael Ross and Fiore Sicoly, "Egocentric Biases in Availability and Attribution," *Journal of Personality and Social Psychology* 37, no. 3 (1979): 322–36, doi.org/10.1037/0022-3514.37.3.322.

7. Elyssa M. Barrick et al., "The Unexpected Social Consequences of Diverting Attention to Our Phones," *Journal of Experimental Social Psychology* 101 (July 2022): 104344, doi.org/10.1016/j.jesp.2022.104344.

8. Beyoncé, "Beyoncé on Her Alter Ego, Sasha Fierce," interview by Oprah Winfrey, *The Oprah Winfrey Show*, Oprah Winfrey Network (OWN), August 17, 2019, youtube.com/watch?v=4AA5G8vCl9w.

9. Rachel E. White et al., "The 'Batman Effect': Improving Perseverance in Young Children," *Child Development* 88, no. 5 (2016): 1563–71, doi.org/10.1111/cdev.12695.

10. Albert Costa et al., "'Piensa' Twice: On the Foreign Language Effect in Decision Making," *Cognition* 130, no. 2 (2014): 236–54, doi.org/10.1016/j.cognition.2013.11.010.

11. Morgan Gianola et al., "Does Pain Hurt More in Spanish? The Neurobiology of Pain Among Spanish–English Bilingual Adults," *Social Cognitive and Affective Neuroscience* 19, no. 1 (2024), doi.org/10.1093/scan/nsad074.

12. Annie Duke, *Quit: The Power of Knowing When to Walk Away* (Penguin Publishing Group, 2022): 188.

13. Igor Grossmann and Ethan Kross, "Exploring Solomon's Paradox: Self-Distancing Eliminates the Self-Other Asymmetry in Wise Reasoning About Close Relationships in Younger and Older Adults," *Psychological Science* 25, no. 8 (June 10, 2014): 1571–80, doi.org/10.1177/0956797614535400.

CHAPTER 4: TALK LIKE COACH

1. Ethan Kross, *Chatter: The Voice in Our Head, Why It Matters, and How to Harness It* (Crown, 2021).

2. Ethan Kross et al., "Self-Talk as a Regulatory Mechanism: How You Do It Matters," *Journal of Personality and Social Psychology* 106, no. 2 (2014): 304–24, doi.org/10.1037/a0035173.

3. Olivia Sappenfield et al., *National Survey of Children's Health Adolescent Mental and Behavioral Health, 2023*, HRSA Maternal and Child Health Bureau report (October 2024), mchb.hrsa.gov/sites/default/files/mchb/data-research/nsch-data-brief-adolescent-mental-behavioral-health-2023.pdf.

4. Ethan Kross and Özlem Ayduk, "Chapter Two—Self-Distancing: Theory, Research, and Current Directions," *Advances in Experimental Social Psychology* 55 (2017): 81–136, doi.org/10.1016/bs.aesp.2016.10.002.

5. Brooks Barnes, "Jennifer Lawrence Has No Appetite for Playing Fame Games," *The New York Times*, September 9, 2015, nytimes.com/2015/09/13/movies/jennifer-lawrence-has-no-appetite-for-playing-fame-games.html.

6. Jake Coyle, "Q&A: Jackman, Hathaway Dream a Dream in 'Les Miz,'" *The Seattle Times*, December 14, 2012, seattletimes.com/entertainment/qa-jackman-hathaway-dream-a-dream-in-les-miz.

7. Rachel Tillman, "Simone Biles Reflects on Decision to Pull Out of Olympics: 'It Was Too Much,'" Spectrum News NY1, September 28, 2021, ny1.com/nyc/all-boroughs/news/2021/09/28/simone-biles-opens-up-tokyo-olympics-decision.

8. Emily J. Oliver et al., "The Effects of Autonomy-Supportive Versus Controlling Environments on Self-Talk," *Motivation and Emotion* 32, no. 3 (2008): 200–12, doi.org/10.1007/s11031-008-9097-x.

9. Leehyun Yoon et al., "Hooked on a Thought: Associations Between Rumination and Neural Responses to Social Rejection in Adolescent Girls," *Developmental Cognitive Neuroscience* 64 (December 2023): 101320, doi.org/10.1016/j.dcn.2023.101320.

10. Nancy Armour, "Simone Biles Wins Something More Important Than Medals at World Championships," *USA Today*, October 8, 2023, usatoday.com/story/sports/columnist/nancy-armour/2023/10/08/simone-biles-world-championships-peace-of-mind/71111240007/.

11. Celina R. Furman et al., "Distanced Self-Talk Enhances Goal Pursuit to Eat Healthier," *Clinical Psychological Science* 8, no. 2 (March 3, 2020): 366–73, doi.org/10.1177/2167702619896366.

12. Paul Rand, host, "The Science Behind Forming Better Habits, with Katy Milkman," *Big Brains Podcast*, University of Chicago Podcast Network, episode 76, September 9, 2021, big-brains.simplecast.com/episodes/the-science-behind-forming-better-habits-with-katy-milkman-57ESaD_G.

13. Phillippa Lally et al., "How Are Habits Formed: Modelling Habit Formation in the Real World," *European Journal of Social Psychology* 40, no. 6 (2010): 998–1009, doi.org/10.1002/ejsp.674.

14. Martin Hyde, "Opinion: Martin Hyde Apologizes for Confrontation with Sarasota Police Officer," *Sarasota Herald-Tribune*, February 25, 2022, heraldtribune.com/story/opinion/columns/guest/2022/02/25/former-candidate-martin-hyde-apologizes-after-video-confrontation-threat-sarasota-officer/6936662001.

15. Allyson Henning, "'I Tried to Bully Her': Sarasota Candidate Threatens to End Officer's Career During Traffic Stop, Apologizes," WFLA News Channel 8, February 23, 2022, wfla.com/news/sarasota-county/sarasota-candidate-threatens-to-end-officers-career-during-traffic-stop-apologizes-for-belligerent-and-rude-behavior.

16. Martin Hyde, "'I Tried to Bully Her': Sarasota Candidate Threatens to End Officer's Career During Traffic Stop, Apologizes," recorded by Officer Julia Beskin's body-worn camera, video, February 14, 2022, posted February 23, 2022, by WFLA News Channel 8, YouTube, 16 min., 29 sec., youtube.com/watch?v=SunGGUktKok.

17. Lindsey Streamer et al., "Not I, but She: The Beneficial Effects of Self-Distancing on Challenge/Threat Cardiovascular Responses," *Journal of Experimental Social Psychology* 70 (May 2017): 235–41, doi.org/10.1016/j.jesp.2016.11.008.

18. Jason S. Moser et al., "Third-Person Self-Talk Facilitates Emotion Regulation Without Engaging Cognitive Control: Converging Evidence from ERP and fMRI," *Scientific Reports* 7, no. 4519 (2017), doi.org/10.1038/s41598-017-04047-3.

19. Igor Grossmann et al., "Training for Wisdom: The Distanced-Self-Reflection Diary Method," *Psychological Science* 32, no. 3 (2021): 381–94, doi.org/10.1177/0956797620969170.

20. Ethan Zell et al., "Splitting of the Mind: When the *You* I Talk to Is Me and Needs Commands," *Social Psychological and Personality Science* 3, no. 5 (2012): 549–55, doi.org/10.1177/1948550611430164.

21. James Hardy et al., "To Me, to You: How You Say Things Matters for Endurance Performance," *Journal of Sports Sciences* 37, no. 18 (2019): 2122–30, doi.org/10.1080/02640414.2019.1622240.

CHAPTER 5: BE ON THE BALCONY

1. William Ury, "Go to the Balcony," Speech, Dawson College Graduation Ceremony, Montreal, QC, 2016, williamury.com/nowithconvictionizbedathanyes2plz/wp-content/uploads/Dawson_graduation_speech.pdf.

2. Ury, "Go to the Balcony."

3. Binyamin Cooper et al., "Trapped by a First Hypothesis: How Rudeness Leads to Anchoring," *Journal of Applied Psychology* 107, no. 3 (June 10, 2021): 481–502, doi.org/10.1037/apl0000914.

4. Özlem Ayduk and Ethan Kross, "Enhancing the Pace of Recovery: Self-Distance Analysis of Negative Experiences Reduces Blood Pressure Reactivity,"

Psychological Science 19, no. 3 (March 1, 2008): 229–31, doi.org/10.1111/j.1467-9280.2008.02073.x.

5. Dominik Mischkowski et al., "Flies on the Wall Are Less Aggressive: Self-Distancing 'in the Heat of the Moment' Reduces Aggressive Thoughts, Angry Feelings and Aggressive Behavior," *Journal of Experimental Social Psychology* 48, no. 5 (September 2012): 1187–91, doi.org/10.1016/j.jesp.2012.03.012.

6. Ethan Kross and Özlem Ayduk, "Facilitating Adaptive Emotional Analysis: Distinguishing Distanced-Analysis of Depressive Experiences from Immersed-Analysis and Distraction," *Personality and Social Psychology Bulletin* 34, no. 7 (May 9, 2008): 924–38, doi.org/10.1177/0146167208315938.

7. James Clear, *Atomic Habits: Tiny Changes, Remarkable Results: An Easy and Proven Way to Build Good Habits and Break Bad Ones* (Penguin Random House, 2018).

8. Atul Gawande, "Want to Get Great at Something? Get a Coach," TED Talk, Vancouver, BC, April 2017, 16 min., 36 sec., ted.com/talks/atul_gawande_want_to_get_great_at_something_get_a_coach.

9. Atul Gawande, "Personal Best," *The New Yorker*, October 3, 2011, newyorker.com/magazine/2011/10/03/personal-best.

10. Josh Waitzkin, *The Art of Learning: An Inner Journey to Optimal Performance* (Simon and Schuster, 2008).

11. "Edgar Mitchell's Strange Voyage," *People*, April 8, 1974, people.com/archive/edgar-mitchells-strange-voyage-vol-1-no-6.

12. Quentin Dercon et al., "A Core Component of Psychological Therapy Causes Adaptive Changes in Computational Learning Mechanisms," *Psychological Medicine* 54, no. 2 (June 8, 2023): 327–37, doi.org/10.1017/s0033291723001587.

13. Daniel Yudkin and Tessa West, "How to Tell If You're the Office Jerk," *The Wall Street Journal*, June 11, 2023, wsj.com/articles/office-jerk-how-to-tell-9f69a49f.

CHAPTER 6: SEE THE BIG PICTURE

1. Jun Fukukura et al., "Psychological Distance Can Improve Decision Making Under Information Overload via Gist Memory," *Journal of Experimental Psychology General* 142, no. 3 (2012): 658–65, doi.org/10.1037/a0030730.

2. Fukukura, "Psychological Distance."

3. Marlone D. Henderson, "Mere Physical Distance and Integrative Agreements: When More Space Improves Negotiation Outcomes," *Journal of Experimental Social Psychology* 47, no. 1 (2010): 7–15, doi.org/10.1016/j.jesp.2010.07.011.

4. National Aeronautics and Space Administration (NASA), "The Challenger STS-51L Accident," accessed June 18, 2024, nasa.gov/challenger-sts-51L -accident.

5. House of Representatives, Committee on Science and Technology, *Investigation of the Challenger Accident*, 99th Cong. 2d Sess., H.R. Rep. No. 99-1016. Government Printing Office, 1986, govinfo.gov/content/pkg/GPO-CRPT -99hrpt1016/pdf/GPO-CRPT-99hrpt1016.pdf.

6. Simon Lambrey et al., "Imagining Being Somewhere Else: Neural Basis of Changing Perspective in Space," *Cerebral Cortex* 22, no. 1 (2012): 166–74, doi.org/10.1093/cercor/bhr101.

7. Marina Hyde, "Are We There Yet? Soon We'll All Be on a Road to Nowhere," *The Guardian*, September 3, 2010, theguardian.com/commentisfree/2010 /sep/03/china-traffic-jam-road-to-nowhere.

8. Pankaj Aggarwal and Min Zhao, "Seeing the Big Picture: The Effect of Height on the Level of Construal," *Journal of Marketing Research* 52, no. 1 (2015): 120–33, doi.org/10.1509/jmr.12.0067.

CHAPTER 7: BE YOUR FUTURE SELF

1. Jeff Bezos, "Jeff Bezos Speaks at Amazon India Event," NDTV Profit, streamed live on January 15, 2020, YouTube video, 25:57, youtube.com /watch?v=jzfXlg-wyUU.

2. AMZ Scout, "Amazon Statistics: Key Numbers and Fun Facts," accessed July 31, 2024, amzscout.net/blog/amazon-statistics.

3. Hal Hershfield, "The Benefits of Getting to Know Your Future Self," *The Wall Street Journal*, June 17, 2023, wsj.com/articles/the-benefits-of-getting-to -know-your-future-self-d3246744.

4. Hal Hershfield, *Your Future Self: How to Make Tomorrow Better Today* (Hachette UK, 2023).

5. Bronnie Ware, *The Top Five Regrets of the Dying: A Life Transformed by the Dearly Departing* (Hay House, 2011).

6. Charles Dickens, *A Christmas Carol* (Chapman & Hall, 1843).

7. Saurabh Bhargava and Lynn Conell-Price, "Serenity Now, Save Later? Evidence on Retirement Savings Puzzles from a 401(K) Field Experiment," *SSRN* (March 13, 2022), dx.doi.org/10.2139/ssrn.4056407.

8. Peter Coy, "Why Do So Many Americans Pass Up Bigger Social Security Checks?" *The New York Times*, November 11, 2024, nytimes.com/2024/11 /11/opinion/social-security-age.html.

9. Jens Agerström and Fredrik Björklund, "Temporal Distance and Moral Concerns: Future Morally Questionable Behavior Is Perceived as More Wrong and Evokes Stronger Prosocial Intentions," *Basic and Applied Social Psychology* 31, no. 1 (2009): 49–59, doi.org/10.1080/01973530802659885.

10. Dan Ariely and Klaus Wertenbroch, "Procrastination, Deadlines, and Performance: Self-Control by Precommitment," *Psychological Science* 13, no. 3 (2002): 219–24, doi.org/10.1111/1467-9280.00441.

11. Yuta Chishima and Anne E. Wilson, "Conversation with a Future Self: A Letter-Exchange Exercise Enhances Student Self-Continuity, Career Planning, and Academic Thinking," *Self and Identity* 20, no. 5 (2021): 646–71, doi.org/10.1080/15298868.2020.1754283.

12. Hal Hershfield, "The Benefits of Getting to Know Your Future Self," *The Wall Street Journal*, June 17, 2023, wsj.com/articles/the-benefits-of-getting-to-know-your-future-self-d3246744.

13. Hal Hershfield et al., "Increasing Saving Behavior Through Age-Progressed Renderings of the Future Self," *Journal of Marketing Research* 48, no. SPL (2011): S23–37, doi.org/10.1509/jmkr.48.SPL.S23.

14. Mark R. Leary, *The Curse of the Self: Self-Awareness, Egotism, and the Quality of Human Life* (Oxford University Press, 2007).

15. Katherine L. Christensen et al., "Back to the Present: How Direction of Mental Time Travel Affects Perceptions of Similarity over Time and Saving Behavior," *Journal of Consumer Research* 51, no. 4 (2024): 761–74, doi.org/10.1093/jcr/ucae029.

16. Benjamin Hardy, "Who Will You Be in 10 Years? Not Who You Expect," *Psychology Today*, May 24, 2022, psychologytoday.com/us/blog/quantum-leaps/202205/who-will-you-be-in-10-years-not-who-you-expect.

17. Jennifer Z. Gillespie et al., "The Suppression of Negative Emotions in Elder Care," *Journal of Managerial Psychology* 26, no. 7 (2011): 566–83, doi.org/10.1108/02683941111164481.

18. Erin Azar (@ImMrsSpaceCadet), "My number 1 tip is to PLAY IT FOR-WARD!," Instagram reel, January 11, 2024, instagram.com/p/C1-x13ztv9E.

19. Anett John and Kate Orkin, "Can Simple Psychological Interventions Increase Preventive Health Investment?" *Journal of the European Economic Association* 20, no. 3 (June 2022): 1001–47, doi.org/10.1093/jeea/jvab052.

20. World Health Organization, "Diarrhoeal Disease," March 7, 2024, who.int/news-room/fact-sheets/detail/diarrhoeal-disease.

21. Lex Fridman, host, "Chris Voss: FBI Hostage Negotiator," *Lex Fridman Podcast*, podcast, episode 364, March 10, 2023, podcasts.apple.com/us

/podcast/364-chris-voss-fbi-hostage-negotiator/id1434243584?i=
1000603624812.

22. Emma Bruehlman-Senecal and Özlem Ayduk, "This Too Shall Pass:
Temporal Distance and the Regulation of Emotional Distress," *Journal of
Personality and Social Psychology* 108, no. 2 (2015): 356–75, doi.org/
10.1037/a0038324.

23. Stephen R. Covey, *The 7 Habits of Highly Effective People* (Free Press, 1989).

24. Lois M. Collins, "To Arthur Brooks, the Biden Question Is About All of Us,"
Deseret News, July 8, 2024, deseret.com/family/2024/07/08/arthur-brooks
-harvard-biden-running-president-retire.

25. Annie Duke, *Quit: The Power of Knowing When to Walk Away* (Portfolio,
2022).

26. Robert Waldinger and Marc Schulz, "The Lifelong Power of Close Relationships," *The Wall Street Journal,* January 13, 2023, wsj.com/articles/the
-lifelong-power-of-close-relationships-11673625450.

27. Anna Lembke, *Dopamine Nation: Finding Balance in the Age of Indulgence*
(Dutton, 2023).

28. Marcus Aurelius, *Meditations,* trans. Martin Hammond (Penguin Classics,
2014).

CHAPTER 8: STOP TIME

1. Daniel Kahneman, *Thinking, Fast and Slow* (Farrar, Straus and Giroux, 2011).

2. David Rock, "Managing with the Brain in Mind," *Strategy+Business,* no. 56
(2009): 1–10, strategy-business.com/article/09306.

3. Nelson B. Amaral, "How Interruptions Influence Our Thinking and the
Role of Psychological Distance," *Journal of Consumer Behaviour,* no. 20
(2020): 76–88, doi.org/10.1002/cb.1856.

4. Paige Hagy, "The $2 Billion Powerball Winner Is Making the Worst Mistakes
Financial Planners Warn People of After They Come into a Ton of Money,"
Fortune, September 19, 2023, fortune.com/2023/09/19/2-billion-powerball
-lottery-winner-edwin-castro-financial-mistakes-advisors-warn.

BIBLIOGRAPHY

Agerström, Jens, and Fredrik Björklund. "Temporal Distance and Moral Concerns: Future Morally Questionable Behavior Is Perceived as More Wrong and Evokes Stronger Prosocial Intentions." *Basic and Applied Social Psychology* 31, no. 1 (2009): 49–59. doi.org/10.1080/01973530802659885.

Aggarwal, Pankaj, and Min Zhao. "Seeing the Big Picture: The Effect of Height on the Level of Construal." *Journal of Marketing Research* 52, no. 1 (2015): 120–33. doi.org/10.1509/jmr.12.0067.

Amaral, Nelson B. "How Interruptions Influence Our Thinking and the Role of Psychological Distance." *Journal of Consumer Behaviour*, no. 20 (2020): 76–88. doi.org/10.1002/cb.1856.

AMZ Scout. "Amazon Statistics: Key Numbers and Fun Facts." Accessed July 31, 2024. amzscout.net/blog/amazon-statistics.

Anikin, Andrey, Nikolay Aseyev, and Niklas Erben Johansson. "Do Some Languages Sound More Beautiful Than Others?" *Proceedings of the National Academy of Sciences of the United States of America* 120, no. 17 (April 17, 2023): e221836 7120. doi.org/10.1073/pnas.2218367120.

Annie Duke. *Quit: The Power of Knowing When to Walk Away*. Portfolio, 2022.

Ariely, Dan, and Klaus Wertenbroch. "Procrastination, Deadlines, and Performance: Self-Control by Precommitment." *Psychological Science* 13, no. 3 (2002): 219–24.

Armour, Nancy. "Simone Biles Wins Something More Important Than Medals at World Championships." *USA Today*, October 8, 2023.

Aurelius, Marcus. *Meditations*. Translated by Martin Hammond. Penguin Classics, 2014.

Ayduk, Özlem, and Ethan Kross. "Enhancing the Pace of Recovery: Self-Distance Analysis of Negative Experiences Reduces Blood Pressure Reactivity." *Psychological Science* 19, no. 3 (2008): 229–31. doi.org/10.1111/j.1467-9280.2008.02073.x.

Barber, Brad M., Yi-Tsung Lee, Yu-Jane Liu, Terrance Odean, and Ke Zhang. "Learning Fast or Slow?" *SSRN Electronic Journal*, 2014. doi.org/10.2139/ssrn .2535636.

Barnes, Brooks. "Jennifer Lawrence Has No Appetite for Playing Fame Games." *The New York Times*, September 9, 2015. nytimes.com/2015/09/13/movies /jennifer-lawrence-has-no-appetite-for-playing-fame-games.html.

Barrick, Elyssa M., Alixandra Barasch, and Diana I. Tamir. "The Unexpected Social Consequences of Diverting Attention to Our Phones." *Journal of Experimental Social Psychology* 101 (July 2022): 104344. doi.org/10.1016/j.jesp.2022.104344.

Bezos, Jeff. "Jeff Bezos Speaks at Amazon India Event." NDTV Profit. Streamed live on January 15, 2020. YouTube video, 25:57. youtube.com/watch?v=jzfXlg -wyUU.

Bhargava, Saurabh, and Lynn Conell-Price. "Serenity Now, Save Later? Evidence on Retirement Savings Puzzles from a 401(K) Field Experiment." *SSRN* (March 13, 2022). dx.doi.org/10.2139/ssrn.4056407.

Brochet, Francois, Peter Limbach, Markus Schmid, and Meik Scholz-Daneshgari. "CEO Tenure and Firm Value." *The Accounting Review* 96, no. 6 (November 1, 2021): 47–71. doi.org/10.2308/tar-2019-0295.

Bruehlman-Senecal, Emma, and Özlem Ayduk. "This Too Shall Pass: Temporal Distance and the Regulation of Emotional Distress." *Journal of Personality and Social Psychology* 108, no. 2 (2015): 356–75. doi.org/10.1037/a0038324.

Carnegie, Dale. *How to Win Friends and Influence People*. Simon and Schuster, 1936.

Chen, Zhansheng, Kipling D. Williams, Julie Fitness, and Nicola C. Newton. "When Hurt Will Not Heal: Exploring the Capacity to Relive Social and Physical Pain." *Psychological Science* 19, no. 8 (August 2008): 789–95. doi.org/10.1111 /j.1467-9280.2008.02158.x.

Chishima, Yuta, and Anne E. Wilson. "Conversation with a Future Self: A Letter-Exchange Exercise Enhances Student Self-Continuity, Career Planning, and Academic Thinking." *Self and Identity* 20, no. 5 (2021): 646–71. doi.org/10.1080 /15298868.2020.1754283.

Christensen, Katherine L., Hal E. Hershfield, and Sam J. Maglio. "Back to the Present: How Direction of Mental Time Travel Affects Perceptions of Similarity over Time and Saving Behavior." *Journal of Consumer Research* 51, no. 4 (2024): 761–74. doi.org/10.1093/jcr/ucae029.

Clear, James. *Atomic Habits: Tiny Changes, Remarkable Results: An Easy and Proven Way to Build Good Habits and Break Bad Ones*. Penguin Random House, 2018.

Collins, Lois M. "To Arthur Brooks, the Biden Question Is About All of Us." *Deseret News*. July 8, 2024. deseret.com/family/2024/07/08/arthur-brooks-har vard-biden-running-president-retire.

Cooper, Binyamin, Christopher R. Giordano, Amir Erez, Trevor A. Foulk, Heather Reed, and Kent B. Berg. "Trapped by a First Hypothesis: How Rudeness Leads to Anchoring." *Journal of Applied Psychology* 107, no. 3 (March 2022): 481–502. doi .org/10.1037/apl0000914.

Costa, Albert, Alice Foucart, Inbal Arnon, Melina Aparici, and Jose Apesteguia. "'Piensa' Twice: On the Foreign Language Effect in Decision Making." *Cognition* 130, no. 2 (2014): 236–54. doi.org/10.1016/j.cognition.2013.11.010.

Covey, Stephen R. *The 7 Habits of Highly Effective People*. Free Press, 1989.

Coy, Peter. "Why Do So Many Americans Pass Up Bigger Social Security Checks?" *The New York Times*, November 11, 2024. nytimes.com/2024/11/11/opinion /social-security-age.html.

Coyle, Jake. "Q&A: Jackman, Hathaway Dream a Dream in 'Les Miz,'" *The Seattle Times*, December 14, 2012. seattletimes.com/entertainment/qa-jackman-hathaway -dream-a-dream-in-les-miz.

Dercon, Quentin, Sara Z. Mehrhof, Timothy R. Sandhu, et al. "A Core Component of Psychological Therapy Causes Adaptive Changes in Computational Learning Mechanisms." *Psychological Medicine* 54, no. 2 (2023): 327–37. doi.org /10.1017/s0033291723001587.

DeWall, C. Nathan, Geoff MacDonald, Gregory D. Webster, et al. "Acetaminophen Reduces Social Pain: Behavioral and Neural Evidence." *Psychological Science* 21, no. 7 (2010): 931–37. doi.org/10.1177/0956797610374741.

Dickens, Charles. *A Christmas Carol*. Chapman & Hall, 1843.

Dizik, Alina. "The Relationship Between Corporate Culture and Performance: Researchers Find that a Positive Culture Boosts Performance, but Performance Alone Doesn't Create a Positive Culture." *The Wall Street Journal*, February 21, 2016.

Duke, Annie. *Quit: The Power of Knowing When to Walk Away*. Penguin Publishing Group, 2022.

"Edgar Mitchell's Strange Voyage." *People*, April 8, 1974. people.com/archive /edgar-mitchells-strange-voyage-vol-1-no-6.

Fridman, Lex, host. *Lex Fridman Podcast*, podcast, episode 364. "Chris Voss: FBI Hostage Negotiator." March 10, 2023. podcasts.apple.com/us/podcast/364-chris-voss-fbi-hostage-negotiator/id1434243584?i=1000603624812.

Fukukura, Jun, Melissa J. Ferguson, and Kentaro Fujita. "Psychological Distance Can Improve Decision Making Under Information Overload via Gist Memory." *Journal of Experimental Psychology General* 142, no. 3 (2012): 658–65. doi.org/10.1037/a0030730.

Furman, Celina R., Ethan Kross, and Ashley N. Gearhardt. "Distanced Self-Talk Enhances Goal Pursuit to Eat Healthier." *Clinical Psychological Science* 8, no. 2 (2020): 366–73. doi.org/10.1177/2167702619896366.

Gawande, Atul. "The Checklist Manifesto: How to Get Things Right." Metropolitan Books, 2009.

Gawande, Atul. "The Coach in the Operating Room." *The New Yorker*, September 26, 2011. newyorker.com/magazine/2011/10/03/personal-best.

Gawande, Atul. "Personal Best." *The New Yorker*, October 3, 2011. newyorker.com/magazine/2011/10/03/personal-best.

Gawande, Atul. "Want to Get Great at Something? Get a Coach." TED Talk, Vancouver, BC, April 2017. Video, 16 min., 36 sec. ted.com/talks/atul_gawande_want_to_get_great_at_something_get_a_coach.

Gianola, Morgan, Maria M. Llabre, and Elizabeth A. Reynolds Losin. "Does Pain Hurt More in Spanish? The Neurobiology of Pain Among Spanish–English Bilingual Adults." *Social Cognitive and Affective Neuroscience* 19, no. 1 (2024). doi.org/10.1093/scan/nsad074.

Gillespie, Jennifer Z., Patricia B. Barger, Jennifer E. Yugo, Cheryl J. Conley, and Lynn Ritter. "The Suppression of Negative Emotions in Elder Care." *Journal of Managerial Psychology* 26, no. 7 (2011): 566–83. doi.org/10.1108/02683941111164481.

Goldberg, Emma. "The CEOs Who Just Won't Quit: What Happens to a Company—and the Economy—When the Boss Refuses to Retire?" *The New York Times*, May 9, 2024. nytimes.com/2024/05/09/magazine/forever-ceos.html.

Grossman, Igor, Anna Dorfman, Harrison Oakes, Henri C. Santos, Kathleen D. Vohs, and Abigail A. Scholer. "Training for Wisdom: The Distanced-Self-Reflection Diary Method." *Psychological Science* 32, no. 3 (2021): 381–94. doi.org/10.1177/0956797620969170.

Grossmann, Igor, and Ethan Kross. "Exploring Solomon's Paradox: Self-Distancing Eliminates the Self-Other Asymmetry in Wise Reasoning About Close Relationships in Younger and Older Adults." *Psychological Science* 25, no. 8 (June 10, 2014): 1571–80. doi.org/10.1177/0956797614535400.

Grove, Andrew S. *Only the Paranoid Survive.* Crown Currency, 1999.

Grove, Andrew S., and Gordon E. Moore. *1985 Intel Corporation Annual Report,* 1985.

Hagy, Paige. "The $2 Billion Powerball Winner Is Making the Worst Mistakes Financial Planners Warn People of After They Come into a Ton of Money." *Fortune,* September 19, 2023. fortune.com/2023/09/19/2-billion-powerball-lottery-winner -edwin-castro-financial-mistakes-advisors-warn.

Haidt, Jonathan. *The Righteous Mind: Why Good People Are Divided by Politics and Religion.* Vintage Books, 2012.

Hambrick, Donald C., and Gregory D. S. Fukutomi. "The Seasons of a CEO's Tenure." *Academy of Management Review* 16, no. 4 (October 1, 1991): 719–42. doi.org/10.5465/amr.1991.4279621.

Hardy, Benjamin. "Who Will You Be in 10 Years? Someone Else." *Psychology Today,* October 2022.

Hardy, James, Aled V. Thomas, and Anthony W. Blanchfield. "To Me, to You: How You Say Things Matters for Endurance Performance." *Journal of Sports Sciences* 37, no. 18 (2019): 2122–30. doi.org/10.1080/02640414.2019.1622240.

Heffernan, Margaret. *Willful Blindness: Why We Ignore the Obvious at Our Peril.* Anchor Canada, 2012.

Henderson, Marlone D. "Mere Physical Distance and Integrative Agreements: When More Space Improves Negotiation Outcomes." *Journal of Experimental Social Psychology* 47, no. 1 (January 2011): 7–15. doi.org/10.1016/j.jesp.2010.07.011.

Henning, Allyson. "'I Tried to Bully Her': Sarasota Candidate Threatens to End Officer's Career During Traffic Stop, Apologizes." WFLA News Channel 8, February 23, 2022. wfla.com/news/sarasota-county/sarasota-candidate-threatens-to-end-offi cers-career-during-traffic-stop-apologizes-for-belligerent-and-rude-behavior.

Herman, Barbara H., and Jaak Panksepp. "Effects of Morphine and Naloxone on Separation Distress and Approach Attachment: Evidence for Opiate Mediation of Social Affect." *Pharmacology Biochemistry and Behavior* 9, no. 2 (August 1978): 213–20. doi.org/10.1016/0091-3057(78)90167-3.

Hershfield, Hal. "The Benefits of Getting to Know Your Future Self." *The Wall Street Journal,* June 17, 2023. wsj.com/articles/the-benefits-of-getting-to-know -your-future-self-d3246744.

Hershfield, Hal. *Your Future Self: How to Make Tomorrow Better Today.* Hachette UK, 2023.

Hershfield, Hal E., Daniel G. Goldstein, William F. Sharpe, et al. "Increasing Saving Behavior Through Age-Progressed Renderings of the Future Self." *Journal of Marketing Research* 48, no. SPL (2011): S23–37. doi.org/10.1509/jmkr.48.SPL.S23.

Hook, John. "Affective Neuroscience: Jaak Panksepp's 'Rat Tickling Theory of Emotion.'" *BJPsych Advances* (2024): 1–4. doi.org/10.1192/bja.2023.71.

Horstmeyer, Derek. "When Investors Do the Most Harm with Market Timing." *The Wall Street Journal*, May 5, 2023. wsj.com/articles/investing-market-timing -ad3c230a.

House of Representatives, Committee on Science and Technology. *Investigation of the Challenger Accident*, 99th Cong., 2d Sess., H.R. Rep. No. 99–1016. Government Printing Office, 1986. govinfo.gov/content/pkg/GPO-CRPT-99hrpt1016 /pdf/GPO-CRPT-99hrpt1016.pdf.

Hyde, Marina. "Are We There Yet? Soon We'll All Be on a Road to Nowhere." *The Guardian*, September 3, 2010. theguardian.com/commentisfree/2010/sep/03 /china-traffic-jam-road-to-nowhere.

Hyde, Martin. "'I Tried to Bully Her': Sarasota Candidate Threatens to End Officer's Career During Traffic Stop, Apologizes," recorded by Officer Julia Beskin's body-worn camera, video, February 14, 2022, posted February 23, 2022, WFLA News Channel 8, YouTube, 16 min., 29 sec. youtube.com/watch?v=SunGGUktKok.

Hyde, Martin. "Opinion: Martin Hyde Apologizes for Confrontation with Sarasota Police Officer," *Sarasota Herald-Tribune*, February 25, 2022. heraldtribune .com/story/opinion/columns/guest/2022/02/25/former-candidate-martin -hyde-apologizes-after-video-confrontation-threat-sarasota-officer/6936662001.

John, Anett, and Kate Orkin. "Can Simple Psychological Interventions Increase Preventive Health Investment?" *Journal of the European Economic Association* 20, no. 3 (June 2022): 1001–47. doi.org/10.1093/jeea/jvab052.

Kahneman, Daniel. *Thinking, Fast and Slow*. Farrar, Straus and Giroux, 2011.

Knowles, Beyoncé. "Beyoncé on Her Alter Ego, Sasha Fierce." Interview by Oprah Winfrey. *The Oprah Winfrey Show*, Oprah Winfrey Network (OWN), August 17, 2019. youtube.com/watch?v=4AA5G8vCl9w.

Kross, Ethan. *Chatter: The Voice in Our Head, Why It Matters, and How to Harness It*. Crown, 2021.

Kross, Ethan, and Özlem Ayduk. "Chapter Two—Self-Distancing: Theory, Research, and Current Directions." *Advances in Experimental Social Psychology* 55 (2017): 81–136. doi.org/10.1016/bs.aesp.2016.10.002.

Kross, Ethan, and Özlem Ayduk. "Facilitating Adaptive Emotional Analysis: Distinguishing Distanced-Analysis of Depressive Experiences from Immersed-Analysis and Distraction." *Personality and Social Psychology Bulletin* 34, no. 7 (2008): 924–38. doi.org/10.1177/0146167208315938.

Kross, Ethan, Emma Bruehlman-Senecal, Jiyoung Park, et al. "Self-Talk as a Regulatory Mechanism: How You Do It Matters." *Journal of Personality and Social Psychology* 106, no. 2 (2014): 304–24. doi.org/10.1037/a0035173.

Lally, Phillippa, Cornelia H. M. van Jaarsveld, Henry W. W. Potts, and Jane Wardle. "How Are Habits Formed: Modelling Habit Formation in the Real World." *European Journal of Social Psychology* 40, no. 6 (2010): 998–1009. doi.org/10.1002/ejsp.674.

Lambrey, Simon, Christian Doeller, Alain Berthoz, and Neil Burgess. "Imagining Being Somewhere Else: Neural Basis of Changing Perspective in Space." *Cerebral Cortex* 22, no. 1 (2012): 166–74. doi.org/10.1093/cercor/bhr101.

Leary, Mark R. *The Curse of the Self: Self-Awareness, Egotism, and the Quality of Human Life.* Oxford University Press, 2007.

Leary, Mark R. "Motivational and Emotional Aspects of the Self." *Annual Review of Psychology* 58 (January 2007): 317–44. doi.org/10.1146/annurev.psych.58 .110405.085658.

Lee, Harper. *To Kill a Mockingbird.* J. B. Lippincott, 1960.

Lembke, Anna. *Dopamine Nation: Finding Balance in the Age of Indulgence.* Dutton, 2023.

Liberman, Nira, and Yaacov Trope. "The Role of Feasibility and Desirability Considerations in Near and Distant Future Decisions: A Test of Temporal Construal Theory." *Journal of Personality and Social Psychology* 75, no. 1 (1998): 5–18. doi .org/10.1037/0022-3514.75.1.5.

MacDonald, Geoff, and Mark R. Leary. "Why Does Social Exclusion Hurt? The Relationship Between Social and Physical Pain." *Psychological Bulletin* 131, no. 2 (2005): 202–23. doi.org/10.1037/0033-2909.131.2.202.

Marquet, L. David. *Leadership Is Language: The Hidden Power of What You Say— and What You Don't.* Portfolio, 2021.

Marquet, L. David. *Turn the Ship Around!: A True Story of Turning Followers into Leaders.* Portfolio, 2013.

Mischkowski, Dominik, Ethan Kross, and Brad J. Bushman. "Flies on the Wall Are Less Aggressive: Self-Distancing 'in the Heat of the Moment' Reduces Aggressive Thoughts, Angry Feelings and Aggressive Behavior." *Journal of Experimental Social Psychology* 48, no. 5 (2012), 1187–91. doi.org/10.1016/j.jesp.2012.03.012.

Moser, Jason S., Adrienne Dougherty, Whitney I. Mattson, et al. "Third-Person Self-Talk Facilitates Emotion Regulation Without Engaging Cognitive Control: Converging Evidence from ERP and fMRI." *Scientific Reports* 7, no. 4519 (2017). doi.org/10.1038/s41598-017-04047-3.

National Aeronautics and Space Administration (NASA). "The Challenger STS-51L Accident." Accessed June 18, 2024. nasa.gov/challenger-sts-51L-accident.

National Transportation Safety Board (NTSB). *Descent Below Visual Glidepath and Impact with Seawall Asiana Airlines Flight 214, Boeing 777-200ER, HL7742,*

San Francisco, California, July 6, 2013. Aircraft Accident Report NTSB/AAR-14/01, Washington, DC, 2014.

Oliver, Emily J., David Markland, James Hardy, and Caroline M. Petherick. "The Effects of Autonomy-Supportive Versus Controlling Environments on Self-Talk." *Motivation and Emotion* 32, no. 3 (2008): 200–12. doi.org/10.1007/s11031-008-9097-x.

Pronin, Emily. "How We See Ourselves and How We See Others." *Science* 320, no. 5880 (2008): 1177–80. doi.org/10.1126/science.1154199.

Rand, Paul, host. *Big Brains Podcast*, podcast, episode 66. "The Science Behind Forming Better Habits, with Katy Milkman." University of Chicago Podcast Network, September 9, 2021. big-brains.simplecast.com/episodes/the-science-behind-forming-better-habits-with-katy-milkman-57ESaD_G.

Rock, David. "Managing with the Brain in Mind." *Strategy+Business*, no. 56 (2009): 1–10. strategy-business.com/article/09306.

Ross, Michael, and Fiore Sicoly. "Egocentric Biases in Availability and Attribution." *Journal of Personality and Social Psychology* 37, no. 3 (1979): 322–36. doi.org/10.1037/0022-3514.37.3.322.

Rotblut, Charles. "Is the AAII Sentiment Survey a Contrarian Indicator?" *AAII (American Association of Individual Investors) Journal*, June 2013. aaii.com/journal/article/is-the-aaii-sentiment-survey-a-contrarian-indicator.

Sappenfield, Olivia, Cinthya Alberto, Jessica Minnaert, Julie Donney, Lydie Lebrun-Harris, and Reem Ghandour. *National Survey of Children's Health Adolescent Mental and Behavioral Health, 2023.* HRSA (Health Resources and Services Administration) Maternal and Child Health Bureau report (October 2024). mchb.hrsa.gov/sites/default/files/mchb/data-research/nsch-data-brief-adolescent-mental-behavioral-health-2023.pdf.

Smriti. "What Happened to Digital Equipment Corporation?" *InspireIP* (blog), February 2, 2024. inspireip.com/what-happened-to-digital-equipment-corporation.

Streamer, Lindsey, Mark D. Seery, Cheryl L. Kondrak, Veronica M. Lamarche, and Thomas L. Saltsman. "Not I, but She: The Beneficial Effects of Self-Distancing on Challenge/Threat Cardiovascular Responses." *Journal of Experimental Social Psychology* 70 (May 2017): 235–41. doi.org/10.1016/j.jesp.2016.11.008.

Svenson, Ola. "Are We All Less Risky and More Skillful Than Our Fellow Drivers?" *Acta Psychologica* 47, no. 2 (February 1981): 143–48. doi.org/10.1016/0001-6918(81)90005-6.

Tillman, Rachel. "Simone Biles Reflects on Decision to Pull Out of Olympics: 'It Was Too Much.'" Spectrum News NY1, September 28, 2021. ny1.com/nyc/all-boroughs/news/2021/09/28/simone-biles-opens-up-tokyo-olympics-decision.

Ury, William. "Go to the Balcony." Speech, Dawson College Graduation Ceremony, Montreal, QC, 2016. williamury.com/nowithconvictionizbedathanyes2plz/wp-content/uploads/Dawson_graduation_speech.pdf.

Von, Theo, host. *This Past Weekend with Theo Von.* Podcast, episode 460. "Jordan Peterson." August 29, 2023. podcasts.apple.com/us/podcast/jordan-peterson/id1190981360?i=1000626052367.

Waitzkin, Josh. *The Art of Learning: An Inner Journey to Optimal Performance.* Simon and Schuster, 2008.

Waldinger, Robert, and Marc Schulz. "The Lifelong Power of Close Relationships." *The Wall Street Journal,* January 13, 2023. wsj.com/articles/the-lifelong-power-of-close-relationships-11673625450.

Ware, Bronnie. *The Top Five Regrets of the Dying: A Life Transformed by the Dearly Departing.* Hay House, 2011.

White, Rachel E., Emily O. Prager, Catherine Schaefer, Ethan Kross, Angela L. Duckworth, and Stephanie M. Carlson. "The 'Batman Effect': Improving Perseverance in Young Children." *Child Development* 88, no. 5 (2016): 1563–71. doi.org/10.1111/cdev.12695.

World Health Organization. "Diarrhoeal Disease." March 7, 2024. who.int/news-room/fact-sheets/detail/diarrhoeal-disease.

"Yaacov Trope, Professor of Psychology, Research." New York University. as.nyu.edu/faculty/yaacov-trope.html.

Yoon, Leehyun, Kate E. Keenan, Alison E. Hipwell, Erika E. Forbes, and Amanda E. Guyer. "Hooked on a Thought: Associations Between Rumination and Neural Responses to Social Rejection in Adolescent Girls," *Developmental Cognitive Neuroscience* 64 (December 2023): 101320. doi.org/10.1016/j.dcn.2023.101320.

Yudkin, Daniel, and Tessa West. "How to Tell If You're the Office Jerk." *The Wall Street Journal,* June 11, 2023. wsj.com/articles/office-jerk-how-to-tell-9f69a49f.

Zell, Ethan, Amy Beth Warriner, and Dolores Albarracín. "Splitting of the Mind: When the *You* I Talk to Is Me and Needs Commands." *Social Psychological and Personality Science* 3, no. 5 (2012): 549–55. doi.org/10.1177/1948550611430164.

Zweig, Jason. "Mirror, Mirror on the Wall, Who Knew That Stocks Would Fall?" *The Wall Street Journal,* December 16, 2022. wsj.com/articles/hindsight-bias-investing-11671206329.

Zweig, Jason. "Want to Beat the Stock Market? Avoid the Cost of 'Being Human.'" *The Wall Street Journal,* April 14, 2023. wsj.com/articles/active-vs-passive-index-fund-beat-the-stock-market-58e8db83.

INDEX